AS WE WERE

FAMILY LIFE IN AMERICA
1850-1900

In pictures and text by
BELLAMY PARTRIDGE
and
OTTO BETTMANN

Whittlesey House
McGRAW-HILL BOOK COMPANY, INC.
New York : London

BRIEF ANNOUNCEMENT

Our story in words and pictures offers a pageant beginning back on the farm in the beguiling fifties. It ends with the appearance of a cloud of dust caused by people coming home from a spin in the countryside towards the close of the century.

Territorially we have confined ourselves to the eastern part of the United States, vortex of the industrial age, which was later on to expand to the West and eventually to the South, regions with which we may concern ourselves another time.

Though many of the pictures shown here have never been reproduced since their original publication, no attempt has been made to press them into a strict chronological order. Our story tries to recapture the period as a whole. It depicts modes of living that change but slowly—defying the stringent rules of the calendar. Where dates are important as landmarks and guide posts, they are given all possible accuracy.

THE AUTHORS.

CONTENTS

INTRODUCTION

Love of the land comes very near being a primary instinct of mankind, for there is, after all, no place like home. For untold ages before man had developed the ideal or principle as the proper thing to fight for, he would shoulder his stone hatchet and march off to war in defense of his homeland.

Americans have always been a land-hungry people. The early settlers came here because land was free and plentiful. It was wild land and they had to tame it. For the most part it was covered with trees which they had to cut down. Some of the wood was used to build houses and make homes, to fashion beds to sleep on and cradles for the babies. For the first two centuries after the landing of the original colonists America was almost exclusively an agricultural land, though it lacked the delights of the seed catalogue and the *Farmer's Almanack*.

Because of banding together for protection against the redskinned savages found already in possession of the land, the first holdings were small. But gradually the farms expanded. The stumps came out of the cornfields and cow pastures, and eventually out of the crude roadways which followed the Indian trails or the wandering paths where cows had walked.

The earliest laws adopted by the communities had to do with the land—how it was to be chosen, how much a man could hold, the duties and privileges of ownership, and the manner of disposition on his demise or other surrender of possession. As relations with the Indians improved, largely through their withdrawal or decease, and the huddling in groups was no longer necessary, the colonists rapidly overran the best of the territory. They kept their axes sharp and went on clearing more and more of the land, following the valleys of the earth and hewing their way back from the streams and up the river courses. Every acre that was cleared was added to the homestead and in due time handed down to the next generation. Aside from a little homemade equipment, the real property was the only property the colonist owned, and the fact that he had carved it out of the wilderness gave it an intrinsic value it would not otherwise have possessed.

Families grew, towns grew, colonies grew. The narrow coastal plain along the Atlantic began to feel crowded to the people who were expanding their farms and who regarded a neighbor within ten miles as altogether too close. The time came when a man could no longer enlarge his holdings simply by cutting down trees and clearing land, and if a family felt the need to expand it had to move farther west. Up to this time there had been no western boundary to the New World. Maps are still in existence which show the future sites of Detroit and Chicago as located in the Colony of Massachusetts, and the rich lands of the Ohio Valley were to be had for the asking from the Governor of Connecticut.

Land was at that time the only potential wealth of our country. All one had to do to realize on it was to get the bothersome and practically worthless timber out of the way, clear the land, put up a cabin—and there you were. A man with a home. Landed gentry. Owner of a substantial piece of God's creation. There must have been a peculiar satisfaction in having an entire continent from which to select the piece of land you wanted. And after acquiring it there must have come a great pride of ownership. The longer a man owned it, the harder he worked to develop it, the more obstacles he overcame in the taming and improving of it, the deeper became the emotions of the man in his relationship with his piece of land.

From the Old Country the early settlers had brought with them the ingrained belief that a man's home was his castle. That, of course, was fighting stuff; it gave him the right to defend it against all comers. But love of the land was something else, something that could easily develop into patriotism, and after a man's holding had descended from father to son a few times, a terrific veneration for the land was likely to be generated.

Songs have been written about the simple homely things of farm life, the old oaken bucket, the one-hoss shay, bringing in the sheaves. Seedtime and harvest have been celebrated in innumerable poems and stories. Following the plow or hoeing corn through the burden and heat of a sixteen-hour day are productive of no particularly pleasurable sensations at the time, but they possess the miraculous power of fomenting a bewitching nostalgia once they are over and have retreated a sufficient distance into the past. Perhaps it is the in-between times which furnish the magic memories, the times when the farm boy is caught up with his work, when there is time to go fishing or indulge in any of the other bucolic delights. Possibly it is the psychology of plenty. Nobody goes hungry on the farm. Something is always developing for

THE PIONEER

the larder. In the summer it comes out of the ground, and in the winter it comes from the barn or the cellar. But whatever the rhyme or reason, it is undeniable that life on the old farm—the horse and buggy farm as it existed for half a century before the coming of the automobile—has called up more fond memories than any comparable period of our national existence.

Farm life in America was indeed in its heyday until the coming of the Civil War and the arrival of the machine age precipitated by the great conflict. With the advent of the shop and the factory a strong drift to the city set in from the farms and small towns. Boys and girls from the country districts were drawn as if by magnet. No doubt the easier living in the cities had its appeal. The shorter hours, the amusements, the crowds, and the excitement. To get rich one must go where money was plentiful. Just the idea of seeking one's fortune furnished a powerful incentive. The great mechanical upswing was in its infancy. Opportunity was knocking on

LEAVING HOME. FROM HORATIO ALGER'S "LUCK AND PLUCK"

every shop and factory door. Of course it was the young, the adventurous, who went, and by and large they attained success. For while not every individual became a millionaire, our country grew into the largest and richest industrial empire the world has ever seen. Many were, of course, sidetracked into a static group identified by the wearing of the white collar. But those who were mechanically inclined made—and are still making—a fabulous success of the machine.

However, the pull of the soil had been only temporarily interrupted. Many of the farm-born adventurers who had gone into the urban areas seeking their fortunes turned back to the scenes of their childhood upon attaining success. With their swift transportation they brought the old farm within easy reach of the city; with their gadgets and mechanical masterpieces they gave it all the comforts and conveniences of city living, and without the dirt and the dust, and

ACQUIRING THE OLD HOMESTEAD

the noise and the smells, and without the shoving around and the waiting in queues that is ordinarily incident to urban existence.

All this is not to say that the farmhand, the grubbing clodhopper, no longer exists. He does, and no doubt he always will, though the coming of the harvester, the all-purpose tractor, and the agricultural schools has vastly lightened his load. If the farmer is shiftless he is probably mortgaged up to the top of the chimney, but his dream and his ambition are still to own a little piece of land in the clear.

The love of the American for his land has not grown cold. Not even lukewarm. The boy and the girl who went to the city so that they might wear their best clothes, have now returned enthusiastically to the land so that they can glory in their oldest and most dilapidated garments. Just another case where absence has made the heart grow fonder.

COUNTRY LIVING

Farm life in America was at its best in the mid-century. Agriculture was the bone and sinew of our national existence. To have a farm of one's own and to work it well was the universal ambition. And while in the latter years of the century the popularity of country living declined through new and unseen forces, memories of the peace and security of the life close to the soil persisted, and doubtless always will persist through times of war and times of peace so long as there is an America.

Haydays of the Old Farm

THE AMERICAN FARMYARD—all about it there is a feeling of abundance and plenty. It is the fall of the year after the crops have been gathered. The barns are bursting with hay. The corn-crib is filled to overflowing. The farmer surveys his yard. He is independent, master of his land, symbol of an era close to the American heart. The equipment is in a way ideal. It is primitive, but eminently practical. Either the animal must come to the well for water, or the water must be taken to all the stock in a bucket—and it is easy to see who is going to carry the bucket. With a well just outside the door Mother would have been considered fortunate indeed; for her dishpan and the baby's bathtub now hanging on the fence could be filled without carrying the water too far.

Fireplace and Parlor are the center of home life in New England a hundred or so years ago. A single candlepower lights the table where a seamstress designs a dress and Junior does his homework. It is a goodly family with nine, perhaps ten children, in which reading is relegated to a tiny shelf underneath the medicine bottle. A row of flatirons occupies the space of honor in the center of the mantel piece where they are quickly accessible in case there is anything to be flattened out. The yards of drying apples along the ceiling insure an abundance of pies during the winter. And the pelt over the Dutch oven must be that of a beaver, else it would be nailed to the barn door to cure. A contemporary comment reminds us how comfortably happy people may be with few wants and no luxuries. "From such firesides," it continues, "great and noble men and women have gone forth into the world."

The farmer's work seems never done. When chores are finished he finds new ones waiting, prescribed by the eternal change of the seasons.

The burden is lightened by the fact that each member of the family does his share. The work is seasoned by sprinkling of fun and laughter.

"Now, then, Children, Hold on!" shouts the farmer getting his hayload under way. For the city child visiting the country the ride on the top of a load of hay is an experience never to be forgotten. The smell of the new-mown hay is of itself exciting, and the swaying and lurching on the jittery perch always present the possibility of an overturn. The view of the hayfield, in fact, the view of life itself from such an insecure eminence, is something out of this world. No child who has missed this experience can be said to have lived his life to the full.

CORNHUSKING gave a welcome chance to mingle work with that most tingling of entertainments: courtship. Living far apart, the younger set of one neighborhood had only rare occasions to get together. Cornhusking was one of them. The boys were bashful and the girls played hard to get, and finding the red ear of corn was a hilarious contrivance for promoting an opportunity for a kiss.

CANDY PULLING was one of those things that went on before the young swains, dropping in of an evening, brought what has now become the conventional box of candy. Molasses taffy was cooked in a kettle on top of the kitchen stove and when ready for pulling was served out in gobs of a size to suit the manipulator. There was no better way to get your arms around the lady of your choice than to stand behind her and help to extricate her hands from a wad of taffy which could be as treacherous as the quicksands, though not usually as fatal. This is supposed to be the origin of the phrase about being "stuck on a girl." The object of the pulling was to make the taffy more brittle and more tasty and to lessen the danger of extracting the fillings from your teeth. It was also regarded as fun.

THE VICTORIAN KITCHEN was of course the center of domestic life, and the warmth and the savory smell of cooking food permeated the house. In those days food was simple but filling. The American housewife learned at an early day to do her baking out of the house, especially in summer. For this she used a Dutch oven such as could be built by any handy man, and if a man wasn't handy he had no place on a farm. Here the great American pie could be baked in huge numbers—and huge numbers were certainly needed, for on a farm you were as sure to get pie for breakfast as for dinner and supper. "When a man can no longer enjoy his pie," says the farmer, "the best of life is over."

SANITATION was a city word which had no place in country living. The American farmer, taking his cues from the animals, cared but little for such new-fangled ideas. In many of the farmhouses the windows were nailed shut and were opened only once a year—at housecleaning time. The germ was beginning to be mentioned, but since seeing was believing, its existence was seriously doubted. Once convinced, however, the farmer accepted the germ with a hearty good will, and today his premises are as germproof as a box of antiseptic gauze.

The problem child was practically unknown a generation or two ago. Never in those days did the youngster come to its mother with the query, "What shall I do now, Mother?" Such an inquiry would probably have sent the child into the hayfield with a pitchfork or out to the woodpile with an ax.

THE PIRATE SHIP—SIGHTING THE ENEMY

On rainy days there was the big barn in which to play hide and seek, the dusty beams on which to climb in search of pigeon's eggs and splinters. And if all else failed, there was always the attic. Here, while the hazards were unfortunately fewer, the properties were far more numerous. This was the one place where costumes could be had without even the asking.

Trunks and boxes were full of costumes, and they hung from every nail, tattered and

threadbare, faded by the sun and by frequent visits to the washtub, riddled by moths, but still bagged at the knees and elbows and still imbued with the personality of the former wearer. Play in the attic was not uninterrupted. Frenzied calls from the stairway inquired from time to time if the house were being torn down. In those old days it was not the children who were the problems—it was the parents. And to a large extent they still are.

OUTDOOR PLAYING was the thing if the weather was good at all. There was the orchard with every kind of fruit to encourage a stomach-ache; the cow pasture where one could easily get wet feet in the brook or the boggy spots; the wood lot where trees grew both large and small, where briars were sharp and ubiquitous, and where the pretty ivy all around was so bright and graceful and so delightfully poisonous—especially to little cousins from the city. And then there was chestnutting. By now most of the native walnut has gone into commodes or gunstocks—and those produce no nuts, especially if finished with a marble top. So the sport of chestnutting must be put down with buffalo hunting and the shooting of the dodo bird—though it was fun while it lasted.

HOW TO CARE FOR BABIES was a problem not always easy to solve on the farm. While the great outdoors was the playground of the older children, baby still had to be attended to. With Mother's numerous tasks it is no wonder inventors, forerunners of our own Rube Goldberg, thought of ways and means to alleviate the relentless drudgery. Not only is the fair operator entertaining herself by rocking her own chair, but she is at the same time soothing the infant and churning the family butter, thus freeing her hands for some other useful task. And while its usefulness on the farm is quite obvious, it is not definitely known whether the invention ever went into production on a commercial scale.

THE LITTLE RED SCHOOLHOUSE, so famous an institution in American life—was a place on which the children lavished no undue affection. In spring and fall the classes were largely composed of the younger children since the older ones were needed on the farm. It was during the winter term, with the classes crowded to the limit, that the so-called district school was at its best. But times have changed, and today the little red schoolhouse is occupied as a filling station or a garage, and the children are whisked into town by the school bus to a larger and much better-equipped institution of learning. Only in the backward regions of the country does the district school still survive, and even there the teacher drives to school from the nearest town in her own car, thereby missing the adventure as well as the boredom of "boarding around" among the families of the district.

A VILLAGE PUBLIC SCHOOL—THE YOUNG ORATOR

Why, one cogitates, was the boy orator so favorite a subject for the artist of an earlier day? The little fellow was invariably a bore and a nuisance. The only redeeming feature about his appearance was the possibility that he might forget his lines. And still the little red schoolhouse rang with his voice each Friday afternoon the length and breadth of the land.

THE PEDDLER'S VISIT was a bright spot in the quiet life of the rural districts. For weeks, perhaps months, the household had been saving its rags in anticipation of the event. The rags were taken in exchange for the shoddy goods and the pans of imitation tin which glittered with a thousand eyes as the shrewd old trader threw open the doors of his traveling bazaar. A peddler who visited Nantucket one year when the hats were tiny announced that it now was the fashion to wear two hats, one on the front of the head and the other one on the back, over the bun. He sold many a pair, so anxious were the women to follow the example of the city styles. The Yankee Peddler, he was called, or the Rag Peddler; and one especially slippery trader sought to disarm his customers by painting on the side of his wagon the slogan, "Live and Let Live." By that name he was known all the rest of his life. In addition to the kitchenware, the peddlers carried needles and thread, thimbles and buttons, piece goods and notions, as well as a hundred other household indispensables. Some of them even carried medicines for man and beast. They were real traders and seldom insisted on seeing any money in a deal. Always they were looking for a chance to swap horses, or they would make an offer on anything you would show them, old or new. Just natural-born traders. Live and Let Live!

Holidays

FOURTH OF JULY was among all holidays the one most cheerfully celebrated by children and grownups alike. Ever since the frost had come out of the ground the country people had been toiling industriously. First there was the plowing and preparing the ground for the seed. Then came the planting, and as soon as the little seedlings were up, the weeding and cultivating began. All too soon the haying season was upon them, and by the time the haying was out of the way, the early wheat, the oats, and the rye would be turning, an indication that they would soon be ready to cut. If the farmer was going to take a day off, this was the time to take it. And from far and near the farm families would stream together to celebrate the greatest of our national holidays—the birth of American independence.

The children would have their firecrackers and popcorn to amuse them, but the big event of the day for the grownups would be the oratory, with or without a parade. The function of the parade was of course to get the people on their feet and moving so that they would follow the band to the speakers' stand. The idea was sound enough, though usually all the best space had been taken long before either the parade or the speakers arrived.

Accustomed to working on their feet, these country people would stand for hours listening to the well-rounded platitudes of the orator of the day, usually a politician who would be coming up for reelection in the fall, and though political speeches were frowned upon, there was no reason why an ambitious fellow could not build up a little prestige by making the eagle scream.

The Americans had an almost Athenian passion for oratory. They would go in droves to any place where it was promised that a speaker would make the rafters ring. It is said that the ferries to Brooklyn were jammed every Sunday with crowds eager to hear Henry Ward Beecher preach, though not so eager to follow his precepts.

After the Fourth of July speeches were over, there would be refreshments, and whiskey, and dancing on the green.

A PICNIC was one of the fixtures of a Fourth of July in the country. The object, no doubt, was to get away from the noise and share stale sandwiches with the ants, mosquitoes, and other occupants of the forest glade. The insects were of course delighted, but some patriotic young American was sure to bring plenty of noise right along with him.

And after nightfall there would be a bonfire and fireworks with a grand "set piece" for the finale, showing the American flag, or an eagle clutching a clawful of arrows. Finally there was the slow ride home under the stars, with the children falling asleep on the seats and father himself feeling a bit drowsy, but permeated with enough patriotism to last for another year.

ALLHALLOW EVE, with apple dippings and jack-o'-lanterns, was the next holiday to be noticed in the country districts. This was largely a matter for the children, though they sought to involve their parents as well as the innocent neighbors in their pranks.

Of course there was the usual amount of gate removing and the tipping over of outdoor plumbing, originally supposed to have been done by witches and other beings known to be full of mischief. Occasionally a wagon would be found the next morning astride the rooftree of a barn. Nobody apparently knew how it got there, though it had to be completely dis-assembled before it could be taken down. And the aggrieved farmer would remark to all con-cerned that if the youths would only exert themselves as hard at their work as at their play, they might amount to something—if given time enough.

HOME FOR THE HOLIDAYS

THANKSGIVING, the day commemorating the landing of the Pilgrims, holds the most meaning among all the holidays. It is an occasion for home-coming—a time when those who have left the nest come back and bring with them any grandchildren who may have happened along.

The Pilgrims were a practical folk who did no actual thanksgiving until they had been in America long enough to raise a crop, and so had something for which to be thankful. For many years it was the great annual occasion for family reunions, with the turkey standing in for the fatted calf, though in recent times the big dinner is usually delayed until after the final whistle of the referee in some football game.

THANKSGIVING DINNER

The Victorians, always good eaters, were inclined to play down the religious aspects of the day and build up the gustatory features. The time devoted to prayer was negligible in comparison with that spent around the festive board. Family ties were jealously maintained and sedulously upheld. Thanksgiving was in the main a family feast, with few if any guests who were not in or close to the family circle. Toasting the future was fully as important as giving thanks for past favors, and it was the custom to bring up at these annual gatherings all matters requiring family discussion—beautifying the cemetery lot, erecting a monument, or perhaps wording an epitaph of an absent member—in other words being gay in the good old Victorian way. They seldom managed to get to church on any day but Sunday, and few of them remembered to get down on their knees with a word or two of thanks for a generous providence; but nobody was ever late to dinner, a feast in the preparation of which nearly every member of the family had some part.

CHRISTMAS, in contrast to Thanksgiving, had a hard time establishing itself in the New World. The Puritans disliked it, claiming that it was pagan in origin and opened the road to rejoicing and feasting. However, there was something distinctly American in this idea of exchanging gifts and of showing one's good will and neighborliness. Americans are a generous people. The vastness of their continent is, as Whitman once said, reflected in the generosity of its citizens. Santa Claus, the jovial, benevolent carrier of the Christmas message, has become the true expression of the good old-fashioned Yuletide.

HANGING UP THE CHRISTMAS STOCKINGS is a custom that must have originated in a day when stockings were being worn; that the stockings were sturdy and capacious also seems likely. With the coming of the stovepipe and the radiator, the hanging place has gradually been shifted from the fireplace to the foot of the bed. It is a pretty custom that has long been encouraged in spite of the growing agnosticism and the sophistication of the younger generation.

A CHRISTMAS CELEBRATION IN AN AMERICAN HOME

The interest and excitement created by the approach of Christmas in the early American country home can hardly be imagined today. Almost every present was homemade, requiring days and perhaps weeks of secret workmanship. There were no convenient stores, or perhaps no money to spend in stores. There were no mail-order catalogues, and buying from advertisements was not then developed as it is today. For weeks the country house would be as full of mystery and secrets as a nest of international spies. A knowledge of the arts and crafts was far more important then than today. Needlework for the girls and carpentry for the boys were almost a necessity. And homemade dolls of the period are now numbered among the almost priceless antiques.

CHRISTMAS BAKING gave the American housewife an excellent opportunity to display her culinary prowess. Pies—cookies—cakes. Having children stir the pudding was a far cry from the electrically driven beater. But, whatever the motive power, the children will always want to lick the spoon.

TURKEY SHOOTING was the men's favorite sport on Christmas afternoon. Americans have always been excellent shots. They had to be in the early days as a matter of self-protection. No opportunity was missed to practice marksmanship, and after the Civil War nearly every returned soldier regarded himself as an expert. The guns were still muzzle loaders, though they were no longer built with the flare of the Pilgrims' blunderbuss. The marksman kept his powder dry by putting it in a horn. Turkey shooting is still carried on in a small way today, though it is done with a punch-board or with curious polka-dotted white cubes shaken freely and tossed from a leathern cup.

The Farmer Goes to Town

THE COUNTRY TOWN, however small, must have been a bright spot to the farmer. Days spent behind the plow or the cultivator, looking at the rear end of a horse—or even a team of horses—can become monotonous. The eye craves a change of scene, a new face, another voice, a different dress filled out in a slightly different form—not necessarily a better one, but one that is not quite so familiar. Almost any excuse will do to get one away. Perhaps an imaginary part for a machine, or even a real part. And why not take along a basket and bring back some fresh supplies? R.F.D. was still far off, but a quick trip on horseback would do wonders for a man, even at the cost of having to take along one of the children for company.

A SHOPPING TRIP to the crossroads store was something quite different. That was an occasion for dressing up. Mother took her basket of eggs in place of spending money, and father had a chance to talk with his old cronies, or perhaps to listen to them and find out what was going on in the world. The children, too, enjoyed the change of scene made memorable as well as adhesive by a stick of candy and perhaps some licorice drops.

THE POST OFFICE, while not providing a living, was a desirable adjunct to a store, since it brought in most of the people of the town nearly every day. Farmers who came to town usually took the mail to the neighbors along the way, for there was a feeling even then that the mail must go through. There was, however, no spectacular regularity about it; often the stage coaches which carried the pouches were days and sometimes weeks behind schedule. Nobody seemed to care. There wasn't any great hurry. Life was leisurely. If things didn't come today they might tomorrow. Anyway it was fun to go into the store and ask. You'd always see people there and have a chance for a bit of gossip if that was what you wanted.

All kinds of people ran the old country stores. Some were shrewd and tricky, watering the molasses, sanding the sugar, and weighing thumbs along with the merchandise. Others were experts in wielding a yardstick whose length had only a faint resemblance to the yard. Such practices started a demand for honest measure. Upon the insistence of enraged customers, brass tacks were nailed to the counter to indicate the exact length of a yard. When the clerk tried any monkey business he was quickly admonished that it was all to his own good "to come down to brass tacks." But the ones who developed into the well-known backbone of America were the dealers who gave honest weight and passed no plugged nickels.

Aside from its function as a marketing center, the general store of the early days was perhaps the greatest American forum for free expression and discussion. It would probably not be too much to say that more than one of our early presidential elections was won or lost in the country stores scattered throughout the nation. Somebody was always around to offer an opinion on any subject or to refute one. Sometimes the arguments went on for days. Often they ended with roused tempers, and occasionally they were finished out back with fisticuffs and bloody noses. And even today the country store is still one of the most truly American of all our native institutions.

THE "FAVORITE RESORT" OF GENERAL GRANT WAS THE STORE OF HIS FRIEND, L. S. FELT, IN GALENA, ILL. "HERE THE GENERAL WHILES AWAY HIS LEISURE IN A PLEASANT CHAT WITH HIS ACQUAINTANCES."

THE VILLAGE SMITHY—or "stithy" as it was often called—was not always under a spreading chestnut tree, though it was an indispensable adjunct of country life before the arrival of the self-propelled vehicle. Back in the colonial days the blacksmith was a man of some influence and importance. While the shop was too noisy to rival the store as a gathering place, every man in town as well as every horse went there periodically, thereby making it a strategic point for political missionary work. However, as the country became mechanical-minded and the machine began to supersede the horse, the smith steadily lost caste until at the end he had little more social standing than the gravedigger or the corn doctor. There was truth in the old saying that your horses' feet were no better than your blacksmith. Careless shoeing could produce corns, or pumiced sole, or even the dread naviculararthritis, described by veterinarians as a disease of the hinge which holds together the coffin and the coronet of a horse's foot.

General Greene of Revolutionary fame was himself a blacksmith before going into the army. Henry Ward Beecher often mentioned his pride at being the descendant of a blacksmith. And when Henry W. Longfellow wrote his famous Fourth Reader poem he was eulogizing one of his own ancestors.

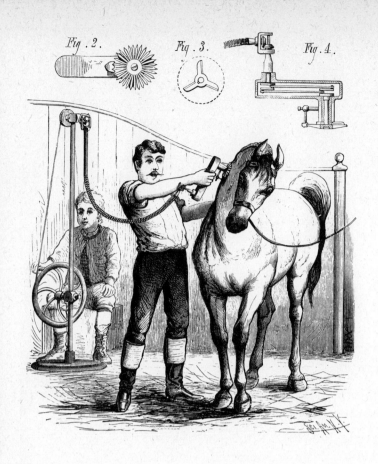

Horses—Horses—Horses! A hitching post or tie rail was in front of every store, emporium, or other commercial establishment in town, and usually there were two posts in front of every house. There was also ample evidence that these were in use. Drinking fountains or troughs abounded at convenient corners in town or forks in the road where there happened to be a spring. No town was too small for a blacksmith shop, a livery stable or two, and the stepping stone out in front was as common as the boot scraper by the door. Any church without a long horse shed could expect few attendants to come from beyond an easy walking distance. Advertisements of spavin cures and liniments lined the roadsides as persistently as the gas and oil signs of today.

Itinerant horse barbers went from farm to farm trimming the fetlocks and often the entire coat of the carriage horses, never failing to finish each job with a call of "Next!"

Having a big appetite and a delicate digestion, the horse requires a good deal of doctoring. Getting him to take the medicine was usually accomplished by the use of long slim wine bottles shoved beyond the swallowing point and held there until empty. A difficult task at best, though one ingenious fellow tried to fool the horse by administering it through a pipe.

THE COUNTRY DOCTOR called on for a wayside diagnosis—what would he have done without a horse? Or the country lawyer who was often called in after the doctor had made his final visit. These old-time servants of the community had little time they could call their own. The doctor must be available night and day, holidays and Sundays. He was not even expected to take a day off to fight a cold or put down an attack of the influenza. The emergency operations of the country doctor, frequently performed on the kitchen table with only the aid of the hired man to hold the patient down and the light of a barn lantern or a kerosene lamp to see what he was about, have saved many a life that might otherwise have been lost before the patient could possibly have been taken to the hospital. And the country doctor was as quickly called out at night to attend a sick animal as a suffering fellow being. If a country doctor was to be successful, he must be a man who couldn't say no. In early New England, which lived in close proximity to its God, disease was long looked upon as a chastisement, or even as the result of witchcraft, a matter that was ordinarily outside the field of the medical man, who was as likely to be the barber or the midwife as the pharmacist. The death of George Washington was undoubtedly hastened by a clumsy bloodletting at the hands of the man who had a barber pole as the insignia of his occupation.

THE ARRIVAL OF THE DOCTOR

For a doctor to be called upon for a wayside diagnosis was not at all unusual, and the experienced medico never went anywhere, not even to church, or to a party, without his little black bag. Exactly what was in it no layman ever knew, and no country doctor was ever known to admit that it did not contain everything that was needed for the case at hand, be the malady or the injury as rare and unusual as it might. Today the country doctor makes his calls in a car, and unless you are on the verge of perishing he gives you nothing stronger than a prescription that you can have filled at the drug store—if you can make your way in between the cigar stand, the lunch counter, the best sellers, and the vast array of perfumes and cosmetics.

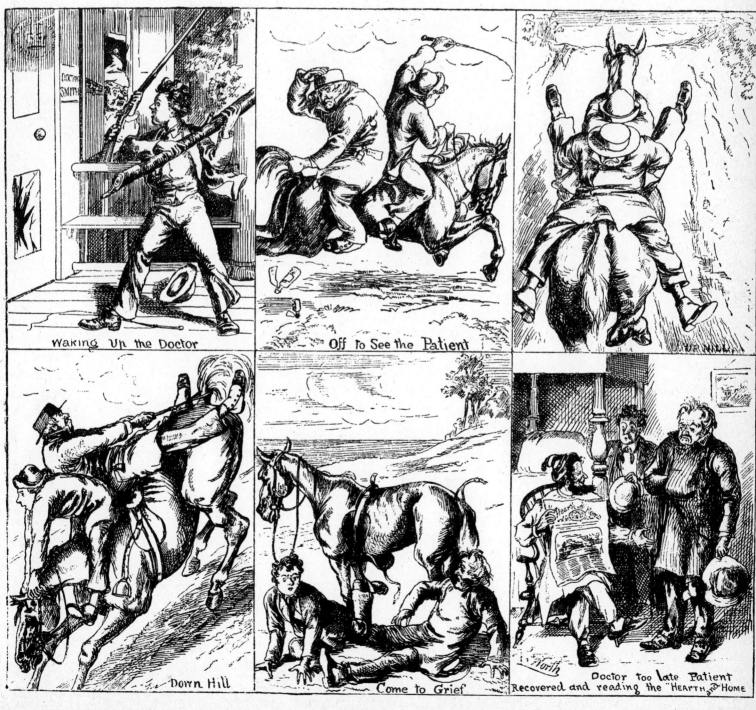

Waking Up the Doctor

Off to See the Patient

Down Hill

Come to Grief

Doctor Too late Patient Recovered and reading the "HEARTH and HOME"

Among the Country Lawyers, of course, there was an occasional scalawag to be found, but taken by and large, so to speak, the most prominent citizen in town was pretty certain to be a member of the legal fraternity. The banker might outshine him in dress and equipage; he might live in a better and bigger house, for the country lawyer rarely amassed any considerable fortune. But nobody ever loves a banker, whereas the country lawyer at one time or another has an opportunity to make almost everybody in town his friend. It is to be admitted that he also has a wonderful opportunity to make enemies. Trying his cases hard and thoroughly makes the other side very angry at the time, but later on when they have a "cause" of their own they are likely to remember the drubbing and want him on their side.

Confidences are a commonplace to the country lawyer, some of them trivial and some positively hair-raising, and there is nothing like a confidence, well used, to establish a basis for a firm friendship. The average country lawyer probably knows more secrets than the parish priest or even the F.B.I. Some of these come to him in his professional capacity, and some are unmitigated gossip. Nobody is in a better position than the country lawyer to sift the false gossip from the true. In many cases he is the only one except the parties involved to know the actualities from the probabilities. It is the use to which the country lawyer puts his inside information which brands him as a useful citizen—or just another he-gossip.

The part played by the country lawyer in obtaining our independence from Britain and putting it in legal form to make it stick has never been appreciated, and his part in building a firm constitutional foundation on which to base our new-born republic has never been sufficiently called to attention. However, the fact remains that twenty-six of the more than fifty signers of the Declaration of Independence were lawyers, nearly all of them from country towns. Of our thirty-two presidents, twenty-three have been members of the legal profession, a large majority of whom came from small towns or even country districts.

In the past half century the importance of the country bar has slumped prodigiously. There are still in the country districts a few of the old-line advocates and counselors, men of high probity and matchless capability who carry on in the best traditions of the profession. But they are mostly oldsters, wedded to their community and too stubborn or too involved to move. But the younger generation, if they are ambitious and have ability, make off to the cities where the fees are large and life in general is much more full of excitement and interest.

The lawyer who drew a will for a dollar or a deed for seventy-five cents is now but a memory, though his signatures are spread liberally over the most sacred, the most vital, and the most historic papers in the archives of our country. His voice no longer rings to the rafters as he appeals to the twelve good men and true, but many of his speeches will be long remembered.

"GENTLEMEN OF THE JURY—"

THE COUNTRY NEWSPAPERMAN of other days, represented in popular magazines, usually leans toward the impecunious editor, who receives his pay for subscriptions in everything except money—as if the subscriptions ever paid for running the paper; or perhaps he is depicted as a stoop-shouldered little fellow about to take a thrashing from an enraged reader who has come, horsewhip in hand, to remonstrate about some item that has appeared in the paper. There was and is nothing puny or pitiful about the editor of the country-town weekly. He was almost invariably able to take care of himself, and if he got the worst of an argument he had the paper on his side and knew how to make the most of it. Usually he was a politician of parts who knew all the right people in the county and possibly the state. And if any of the old-timers have survived until the present day, they are in all probability the owners of newspaper chains, many of which have become rich and powerful.

THE COUNTRY CHURCH was a real power in the heyday of the old farm. It furnished the farm family not only a means of salvation, but a place to go, social life, cheap amusement, and an opportunity for an exchange of news and views. With the coming of the automobile, however, the little white church in the valley is falling into disrepair. In some places its doors are seldom thrown open except for funerals and weddings. The bell in the steeple is silent. Only the weathervane remains active and operative, pointing out the direction of the winds with its accustomed fidelity. But unfortunately in these days when the weather forecast comes in over the radio and no man is called upon to make his predictions for himself, the weathervane swings back and forth entirely unnoticed; and as for the wind—let it blow.

A nineteenth-century parson whose sermon lasted only an hour or less was considered to have done no more than skim the cream from his text. A harangue of an hour and a half was regarded as just a fair job. Sin, it seemed, was pretty well entrenched and could not be driven out by anything less than two solid hours of thundering hell-fire and damnation—and even then the devil would have it back on its feet again in time for the sermon on the following Sunday morning.

DISPLAYING A NEW SEALSKIN COAT was one of the moments of triumph for the wife of a farmer who had made good. The church was the only place where opportunity existed to outdo one's neighbor in the matter of dress. Since all style is relative, the competition must have been as keen as in the Easter Parade on Fifth Avenue, though with slightly different models.

CAMP MEETINGS and other religious assemblies gave the devil very little time for rest and recreation. In winter almost every Protestant church would have a week or two of "revivals," staged in the crowded meetinghouses around the red-hot stove where the devil was given his due nightly and the backsliders and sinners were high-pressured into the fold. The camp meeting which came in the summer was conducted under far less emotional stress, for it combined the business of saving souls with the fun of camping out. People drove to the camp meetings from miles away. The entire congregation of a church would assemble, and having been packed in their wagons along with tents, provisions, and camping equipment, would travel in a train like a band of gypsies, with a pall of dust hanging over them until they had reached the appointed meeting place, usually a piece of woods with a near-by brook or other dependable water supply. Here they would foregather and make their camp.

Once or twice daily and perhaps oftener they would hold their religious meetings, which were often of a revivalistic nature. They were hailed by the ungodly as gatherings which were not strictly for religious purposes, and it is true that many scandals resulted, though these were usually hushed up for the good of the cause.

A story credited, along with the others to Abe Lincoln, tells of a young man who, when signing his enlistment papers for the Civil War, was unable to give his father's name. When pressed for an explanation by the sergeant in charge, the applicant shook his head sadly and replied, "Reckon I was just one of them camp-meeting babies."

LOVE-MAKING AMONG THE TENTS

THE COUNTRY FAIR was another of those institutions creating excitement in the hearts of old and young—not familiar to the citizens of an age in which entertainment is to be had any minute of the day by the turn of a radio dial. The earliest fair known to have been held in America was put on by the American Institute in New York City in the eighteen twenties. This, how-  ever, was largely industrial, though in addition to a fine display of flowers raised in the back-yards there were pumpkins grown in abundance on farms in Harlem, and stock fattened in the neighborhood of what is now Madison Square came off with a number of blue ribbons. The idea of local agricultural shows where neighbors could vie with one another and compare the size and quality of their turnips and winter squash was brought over by the Pilgrims along with their New England consciences and their ladderback chairs. Beating the other fellow is something that goes back to the delightful period known as time immemorial.

That horse racing has long been associated with the country fair is undeniable, though the origin of the entertainment is in doubt. It might well have started from the haste of the farmers to get home for the evening chores. And after a few of these highway brushes which, as often as not, ended in the ditch, some member of the fair committee with a gift for promotion may have tempted the owners of fast horses with prize money and moved the races inside the fair grounds.

North Guilford Martial Band

The Merry-Go-Round came in after the country fair had become more a carnival and less an institution for the betterment of agricultural products. Nor were the children the only ones devoted to the riding of the wooden horses and other curious beasts of burden. Games of chance also crept in, wheels of fortune, raffles, and various other means of winning a little while losing a lot. Eventually there was as much pink lemonade at the country fair as at the circus, and the country folk went home loaded with free literature about everything from spavin cure to lightning rods. Even the shell game used to thrive at the country fair, though it had to be run surreptitiously and could not be too rapacious about robbing the customers.

GUESSING AT THE WEIGHT of animals was one of the popular contests of the country fair. This little game, discussed by its participants with all the earnestness and zeal of a world problem, grew out of the scarcity of weighing devices. Platform scales, if they existed at all, were few and costly. Many a complicated formula, largely derived from measurements, was devised to enable the stock raiser to figure the probable weight of his animal so that he could compute its worth without waiting for it to be cut up by the butcher. At the country fair the homey Pythagorases had a chance to put their theories to the test.

Though the decision of the judges and the awarding of the ribbons were final and beyond any hope of appeal, the unofficial opinion of onlookers often led to discussions and disagreements over the respective merits of exhibits, the comparative weights, or perhaps the pulling power. Sometimes these differences of opinion led to contests not on the program and disputes settled behind the animal sheds, with a bit of wagering on the side.

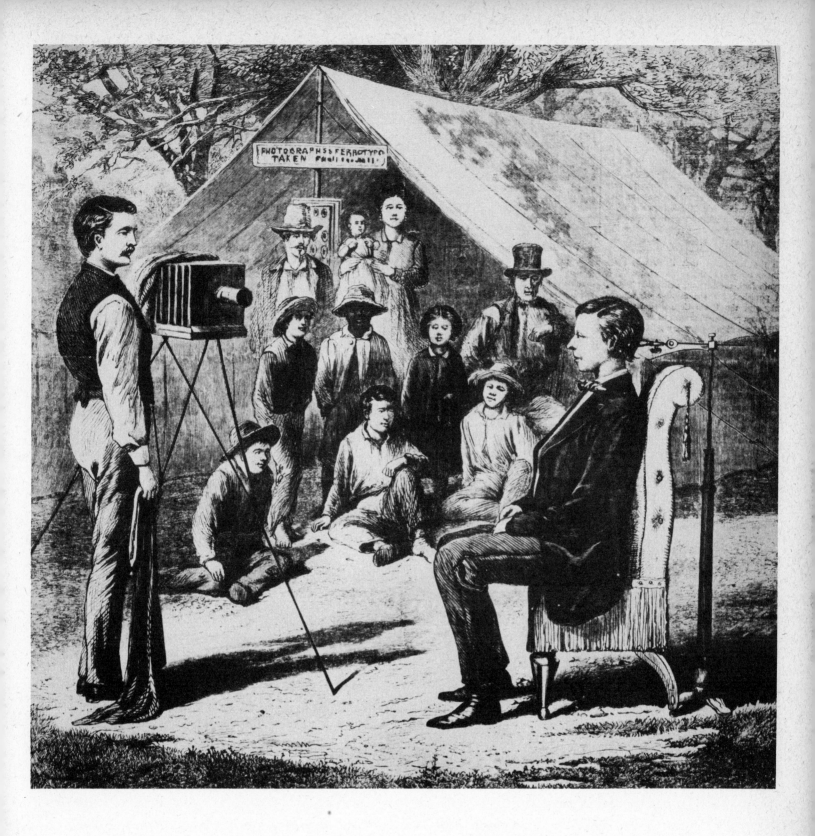

THE TENT OF THE TRAVELING PHOTOGRAPHER was an indispensable adjunct to any fair. The vanity of the human race, like Tennyson's brook, goes on forever. In the days of the old wet plates and the slow time exposures, merrymakers out for some fun would be easy to persuade to make a sitting. And even today with the roller coaster, the river of love, the house of mystery, and the pinball machine, the picture-taking game is as popular as ever, only now the sitter drops a coin in the slot and takes a dozen instantaneous views of himself at a time. And we say as in Ecclesiastes, "Vanity of vanities . . . all is vanity." Times may change but vanity is everlasting.

THE RETURN FROM THE FAIR

The fun was over. The curtain was about to ring down. The horses were restless, the children exhausted, and Mother's feet hurt. And once the family were in their own conveyance, the horsewhip came out of the socket. Perhaps it was just the dust. Perhaps it was the excitement. Possibly it was nervous tension after a day at the fair.

Or it may have been the fact that although people came stringing in a few at a time they all wanted to go home together. It was an exodus that never failed to border on a stampede. Much the same thing goes on today, only now we do it with motor cars at sixty or better.

THE GREAT DIVIDE: CIVIL WAR

The bloody story covering the Civil War has been told and retold. Its personalities who have enriched our national past have become well known to us through their large two- and three-volume sets of memoirs they themselves produced, and latterly through the large and extensive biographies by which they have been explained, interpreted, evaluated, and assessed by others.

Tough and debatable subjects such as slavery, secession, state rights, emancipation, and the like have been covered and recovered in a multitude of learned treatises. Stories of camp life and battlefield have been repeated by the returning soldiers on both sides until they have become as well known as the tales of Mother Goose. Tactics and strategy of every battle are better known and understood today than they ever were by the generals who directed them, all these engagements having been analyzed and studied at West Point for three-quarters of a century.

We are not now concerned with marching men, however, their strategy, their victories, or their defeats. These having been adequately and often admirably dealt with both in words and in pictures, our main emphasis is on the effect of the war on the body politic, on the people. Here we are dealing with the home front. We face the first and most painful meaning of the war—men must go and fight. They must put on uniforms, and what uniforms. They must part with their loved ones and leave behind all they held dear in an age when sentimental farewells were rampant. They must learn to subsist on salt pork and hardtack, to sleep on a plank or on ground as hard as one. And they must march and march and march, which in those days they did on their feet. We see the women engaged in war work. They are making ammunition—in one-room factories, serving in flower-decked canteens, and taking the place of male office workers who have thrown up their jobs and marched off to war to the martial strains of Yankee Doodle. Not yet are the women in uniform. That would be going a little too far; but the Treasury Department in Washington is full of them, clad in voluminous silks and satins, the printing and counting of money being regarded as suitable employment for the most genteel of women.

But the war is producing results not immediately apparent, results that are to have wider repercussions in America than the Emancipation Proclamation. Forces only faintly discernible before the war are brought suddenly into the foreground. Industry called upon for the emergency production of arms and munitions hastily mobilizes the industrial forces in the cities, where workers will be more readily available. Almost before the country realizes what is going on it is in the midst of a second revolution, an uprising that is to lead from the civil conflict between state and state to a great reunited industrial domain. Out of the ruins of war a new America is to emerge—and a new American.

A vast shift of the population begins from the land to the city, from the farm to the factory. The individual craftsman takes a factory job and thus paves the way for mass production; and the city sends back to the farm a machine to take the place of the men it has hired away.

In the new industrial setup little businesses were turned into Big Business with such enthusiasm that nobody thought of the evil days ahead when trusts would have to be busted, concentrations of capital unscrambled, and excess profits turned over to the government to keep the rich from becoming too rich while the poor were becoming only moderately rich. Mines, mills, and factories boomed. And America entered upon a new way of life where people went to work when the whistle blew.

FILLING CARTRIDGES AT THE UNITED STATES ARSENAL

Doings on the Home Front

Northern industry had developed to a point where it could be very quickly and effectively converted to the manufacture of munitions. Women filled the place of men called to the colors. The demands of war made them indispensable on the farm, in the office, and in the factory.

The South, almost completely lacking in such large-scale facilities, still in the workshop or hand-production stage, was greatly hampered in arming and equipping its armies in the field. Many of its units were not better armed than some of the American forces at Bunker Hill who had gone to war with pitchforks and sickles.

WOMEN WORKING IN THE FIELD

ASTOR HOUSE CHEFS, OHIO BEEF, AND ILLINOIS PORK FALL IN LINE PROVIDING THE SOLDIERS WITH FOOD

SEWING CIRCLE WORKING FOR THE SOLDIERS

THE NEW TAX LAW OF 1862 made the home front feel the impact of war. Old taxes were increased and numerous new ones were created: stamp taxes, inheritance taxes, taxes on buildings, and even on slaves. The artist who drew the picture above was much impressed with the "lamb-like docility with which the victims went up to be shorn" of their surplus wealth at the New York Assessor's Office.

CLERK STAMPING THE LICENSE

The Working Men's Savings Bank!

People with War Savings Bonds drawing an average of 2.5 per cent interest and Treasury Savings Notes bearing as little as 0.6 per cent will raise their eyebrows at the 7 per cent thirty-year loans of Civil War days. Working men were urged in posters and handbills to "fetch on" the little sums of fifty and one hundred dollars and "make the U.S. Government your savings bank." Jay Cooke, the Philadelphia banker, was made sole agent for the "Five-Twenties" authorized in February 1862. Somewhat different from the late war when war bonds and stamps could be bought in nearly every five-and-ten.

The South, too, was digging into the old sock or mattress, though it was offering only 6 per cent interest.

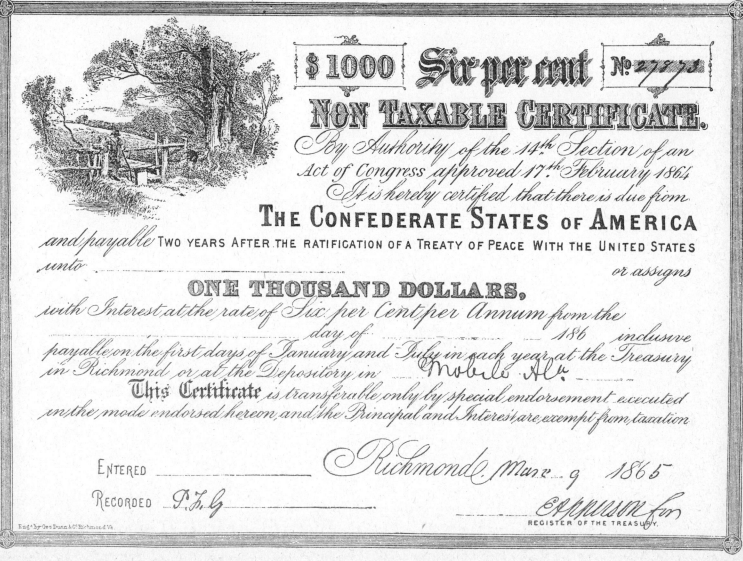

LADY CLERKS were employed at the Treasury Department. Putting an army of a million men into the field increased the demand for women office workers in Washington, a demand which was eagerly filled, partly because of the close proximity of the Nation's capitol to various Army camps. Fashion had not yet caught up with the demands of the working girl. Women swept the streets of Washington with their tremendous hoops. The Secretary of the Treasury put a walking board across the muddy street so as to save his faithful helpers from sinking in knee-deep. How these girls managed in the crowded omnibuses of wartime Washignton is somewhat of a riddle—and a consolation for modern commuters.

OFFICE IN THE TREASURY DEPARTMENT

There were those who ridiculed the idea that a woman, especially a pretty woman, could be of any practical worth in an office, especially a government office.

Some of the masculine alarmists went so far as to predict that if the trend continued, women would one day don the uniform and might even become officers, a thought almost too terrible to contemplate.

COSTUME A LA GRANDE MILITAIRE

SOUTHERN BELLES, though not working in factories, furthered the cause of the Confederacy by making clothes for their soldiers—at the same time putting pressure on their beaux to get out and shoulder a musket.

Rationing Boards had been established by the Federal government in the no-man's-land which lay between the two armies. Impoverished whites as well as the negroes were compelled to call on the Union forces for subsistence. This was especially true as the war continued and the South became poorer and poorer while the war prosperity in the North made the country north of the Mason-Dixon line seem richer and richer. United States commissaries which had been set up at essential points were besieged by the rich and poor alike. It was not at all unusual to see a stately Southern lady of the aristocracy standing in line before a counter, waiting to get her household ration of salt fish and hardtack. She took it because she needed it to keep herself and her family from starving. But she accepted it without any lessening of her pride or her dignity.

Provisions were made for feeding the colored people apart from the white, though colored servants were permitted to enter the place reserved for the whites in order to draw rations for their mistresses, who were often too ill or perhaps too proud or too bitter to come in person.

Great wars create great heroes—they also offer great opportunities for racketeering. The soldier "slugging it out"—deprived of comfort and in constant danger—is justly bitter toward the home front oblivious of its duty. Bitter, yet just, gripes from those who do the fighting are a familiar reaction.

During the Civil War, profiteers, with special emphasis on the war contractors, became so bold and greedy that they were openly attacked in the press, especially for the fraudulent material used in the uniform cloth and known as "shoddy."

THE CONTRACTOR

A "shoddy aristocracy" sprang up, best known for its reckless buying of costly luxuries and its pretentious vulgarity.

THE CONTRACTOR'S WIFE

The sixties treated the home guard, grandfather of the armchair strategist, with sarcastic scorn.

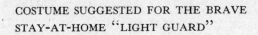
COSTUME SUGGESTED FOR THE BRAVE
STAY-AT-HOME "LIGHT GUARD"

LADIES IN ATTENDANCE IN
REGULATION COSTUME AT
THE METROPOLITAN FAIR

Though there were no government-inspired or government-conducted societies or organizations to improve the lot of the soldier in the field and to bring him comforts and recreations beyond the ability of the Army to furnish, various relief societies sprung up in every city, town, and hamlet, raising during the course of the war some seventeen million dollars. All these activities were eventually coordinated under the name of the Sanitary Commission. Trained agents who were placed in charge of the distribution of supplies raised by the commission accompanied every movement of every Union army. The word "sanitary," derived from an interest in preventive hygiene among the fighting men, was adopted for household use, and everything sent to the soldiers, from a glass of currant jelly to a pair of red flannel underdrawers, went by the name of sanitary stores.

All the usual methods of raising money were employed at the Sanitary Fairs, from the sale of donated articles and merchandise to that of the exquisite pleasure of scrutinizing a lady's skin through a magnifying glass.

EPISODE IN OPTICS: ONLY TEN CENTS

SOLDIERS' BALL AT HUNTSVILLE, ALABAMA—DANCING THE "VIRGINIA REEL"

PARADE OF RETURNING SOLDIERS, 1865

The wise saying that the harder the conflict the more glorious the triumph was probably never more clearly illustrated than at the end of the Civil War, in the North. An enthusiastic citizen in New York proposed that a table be spread the entire length of Broadway from the Battery to Union Square, at which the returning soldiers were to be banqueted. Needless to say, the idea was not adopted. The fact was that the soldier boys were so anxious to get home that they did not want to stop even to eat, and a committee was formed to take baskets of food to the trains so that they could eat as they went along.

Government estimates that demobilization could be completed in three months proved to be wide of the mark, and though much of the work was left to private initiative, complete disbanding of the forces required a full eighteen months. However, the ease with which the veterans were absorbed back into civil life causes even more surprise today than back in the sixties. To quote a slightly mixed metaphor of the time, their return caused "rarely a ripple on the surface of the social fabric."

THE BOYS ARE COMING HOME AGAIN

Postwar World

Sword I'm turning into plowshare,
Into reaping hook the gun,
Here are bayonets by the bushel—
Shall I shoe your horse with one? . . .

A returning army is always an army of changed minds. The serious business of soldiering produces sober thoughts. The fighting man has been seeing and doing things which give him a new vista of life. With his new thoughts he wants new things. This time the returning soldier found the home front almost miraculously changed. National aims had quite definitely done an about-face. The experience of the war effort had given heavy industry a terrific upswing. Iron and steel were booming. Railroads, which had an ominous beginning decades before the war, started to link the nation together. Manufacturing and business and the invention and distribution of labor-saving devices absorbed a good deal of the returning manpower. The machine age was upon us and tremendous changes were in the making. Life and leadership had reached a crossroad. It was America's great moving day.

FROM FARM

FROM STAGECOACH

FROM MAIN STREET

TO FACTORY

LOOK OUT FOR THE LOCOMOTIVE

TO RAILROAD

TO BROADWAY

ADVERTISING, 1865, OF THE ILLINOIS CENTRAL RAILROAD OFFERING SETTLERS LAND ON CREDIT AND AT LOW PRICES

The West was thrown open for further development, with special inducements to the veterans, many of whom wanted to go into machine farming in a big way as soon as the mechanical reapers and harvesters were ready. Many of them were anxious to spend their bonus money for a farm in the West. The railroads, blessed with fabulous land grants, encouraged settlements along their lines and described the new Eden in luring terms.

WINDSHIP WAGONS seemed to be the best means of traveling over the prairies. The settlers from the East being at heart inventors and gadgeteers had dreams of many a curious contrivance. Before railroads spanned the continent, Uncle Sam was also doing a bit of daydreaming when he experimented with the use of camels to get freight shipments across the deserts of the Southwest.

THE BUILDERS OF THE PACIFIC RAILROAD were more practical, and thousands of the returning soldiers went into the West to help extend the steel rails across the plains. This building project proved to be one of the great engineering achievements of the century and was the most impressive postwar employment project ever conceived up to that time.

In the case of the railroad, as with every other improvement in public transportation, there were enthusiasts on the one side, obstructionists on the other—old-fashioned people who wanted to let well enough alone. It was so when the stage coach superseded the pillion, when the horsecar was replaced by the trolley, and it was especially so when steam superseded the picturesque sailing ship. Here the seafaring men resisted not only with their arguments but with their fists. But the resistance was in vain. The machine-driven craft won the day. Resistance was equally vain when the railroad proposed to take over all long-distance land travel.

LIFE INSURANCE CLOTH FOR TIMID RAILROAD TRAVELERS

Objection was made to the noise, the speed, the danger. The smoke and gases, it was said, would poison the air so that wild birds and vegetation along the tracks would be destroyed. Hens would not lay. Horses and cattle would starve. The fear of boiler explosion was prevalent —and not wholly unjustified. Boilers did explode, and when they gave way serious damage was likely to follow. Ridicule was the answer to the timid travelers, and while some of the early railroads piled bales of cotton in a car behind the engine to reassure the traveler, they also improved their rolling stock so that the traveling became safe and enjoyable. As the century moved along, the parlor car and sleeper were built so that they offered all the comforts of home —including organs and opportunity for social gatherings.

PALACE-CAR LIFE ON THE PACIFIC RAILROAD

PILGRIMS OF THE PLAINS were on the move—an endless caravan, many of them "Boys in Blue." They spread over the fertile plains. Most pioneers of course did not travel by train. They moved by boat and covered wagon; however, without the railroads to bring in supplies and provide facilities for the flow of goods, the settling of the great West could never have succeeded. It was a new and sturdy generation of pioneers that settled in the new Border States, Minnesota, Dakota, and Nebraska. . . .

. . . and Kansas—a State richly endowed by railroad grants welcomed the new settlers—and land offices did a land-office business.

In the decade after the Civil War, agriculture especially was subjected to a change of truly revolutionary proportions. The Eastern farmer did not hail the arrival of the new mechanized equipment with any undue enthusiasm but went about the gathering of his pumpkins in the accustomed way.

In the West, however, the progressive settler, aided by all the latest machinery, went into his agriculture in a big way and rapidly developed the fertile plains beyond the Mississippi. This expansion had its setbacks. However, in time the West emerged as the bread basket of America and of the whole world. While land-office records do not tell us how many of these settlers were veterans, there is no doubt that they had a great share in developing the new regions.

THE VILLAGE DEPOT

It was not long before the railroad had become the focal point of community life. Towns fought to be included on the right of way of a projected line, offering free land for the erection of freight and passenger facilities, as well as unlimited space for storage and yardage of rolling stock. But in spite of the liberality of the towns and cities, the farmers, especially in the East, were not so cooperative. Indeed, so far as they could they resisted the building of railroads through or along their property because of the danger of setting fire to their crops, and the frightening of their animals. They got along all right, they said, before the railroad was ever thought of, and they were perfectly willing to go on just as they were. Agricultural sidings for the loading of crops did not especially interest them—not at that time, but would they be sorry later! Fortunately progress is not stayed by the stubbornness of a few short-sighted men, and the roads went through. There were a few hardshells who stood off and refused even to ride on one of the trains. The next generation, however, made up for all that.

Going to meet the trains was something to do on a dull day, and between trains the depot—or station as it was later called—made an ideal trysting place. It was shaded in summer and heated in winter, and a lot of things went on there that the station agent knew nothing about. It was a convenient place for the exchange of notes between those whose love affairs were meeting with objections at home. A girl could always find plenty of excuses to account for a visit to the station. Her letter might have reached the post office just too late to get into the mail pouch, so she would have to take it over and put it on the train. She could always be expecting one of her girl friends to be returning from a neighboring town. And she could, on a pinch, go down just to see the train come in. Certainly there could be no harm in that. And she could have stepped inside the station just as a certain boy was coming out the door—and if she suddenly found a note in her hand—well, what of it?

THE CONVERTERS

WATCHING THE CONVERTERS

Casting ingots.

Heating ingots

BESSEMER STEEL MANUFACTURE

The railroad was largely back of heavy industry, not only because of the use of so much iron and steel in its own structural work, but because it was always pressing farther and farther with its development of the country and the opening of new territory. Back in the seventies the making of Bessemer steel was really hot news.

STUDENT'S LAMP

The new industries springing up during the Civil War were important not only as examples of American business acumen and sources of income for stockholders and tycoons. These enterprises made for a new and better life for the average family, giving them modern comforts and conveniences.

Until the middle of the nineteenth century the American home depended for its light on the tallow dip and whale oil. The tallow candle was cheaper. It was something that could be made at home if one wanted to take the time and the bother. Sperm oil was for the well-to-do. It was smelly stuff, but it gave a good light. Indeed, John Quincy Adams hailed this illuminant as the "non plus ultra" of light-producing agencies. Then suddenly a new oil came into the picture. It was made of something that came out of the

WHALERS GAUGING OIL

ground in Pennsylvania. After it was processed they called it "coal oil" or "kerosene." This new oil was inexpensive, but it was dangerous. Unless used with care it would explode, producing a great deluge of liquid fire. The insurance companies fought it, and for many years the railroads refused to use it either in their switch and signal lights or in the lanterns of the workmen who ran the trains at night. As lamps were improved, whaler crews found themselves out of a job. They made haste to reach the oil fields of Pennsylvania.

ON THIS PICTURE, **LOOK** THEN ON THIS.

COMMON KEROSENE OIL.   SILVER LIGHT ASTOR OIL.

There was much talk too during the Civil War of a coming age of dream kitchens and labor-saving devices.

THE SEWING MACHINE was a primitive affair before the conflict. It was run by a hand crank, but it would sew much faster and easier than the human hand using a needle and thread. Its introduction bore out the same old story. It was criticized and obstructed by the very persons whose labor it was designed to save. Women refused to wear dresses with machine stitching. And the men scoffed at suits that were not sewn by the hand of a man tailor. Clothing manufacturers made a determined effort to popularize their machine-made clothes but they were stymied in their efforts until the government took up the sewing machine as a means of providing the Union armies with uniforms with the least possible delay.

The machines, bought by the government, were loaned free to sewing circles or individuals who were willing to turn out uniforms for the soldiers as a patriotic duty. It was thus that the government accomplished what private enterprise had been unable to do. It familiarized thousands of housewives with the use of the sewing machine as well as clothing the soldiers with what were then the best uniforms in the world. From that time on no American family could get along without a sewing machine in the house. And as for hand-sewn clothing—where is it now?

SECURING AN OUTFIT

SAILORS' OUTFITTING STORE

The American soldier always wears his uniform with pride, but once the job is done he goes back to his civilian clothes with great enthusiasm. Soldiers returning after Appomattox, however, found themselves facing a situation quite different from that which prevailed when they went to war. During their absence really good readymade clothing had arrived. The manufacturing tailors had been forward-looking and had taken advantage of their experience in the making of thousands of uniforms as well as collecting valuable data on sizes and measurements which had never before been available to them. Ready-to-wear clothes had been struggling to find a market since the invention of the sewing machine but had never been able to satisfy the American man who preferred to have his clothes made to order even if he had to wait two or three weeks to get a suit.

All this was changed after the war when the men came back and found a fine selection of well-made civilian clothes ready to put on without any delay at all. Accustomed to wearing the machine-made uniform in the field they had lost much of their prejudice against the ready-to-wear and quickly took advantage of the opportunity to get out of uniform, though they did, for a time, insist on having the creases pressed out so that nobody would recognize the clothes as being readymade.

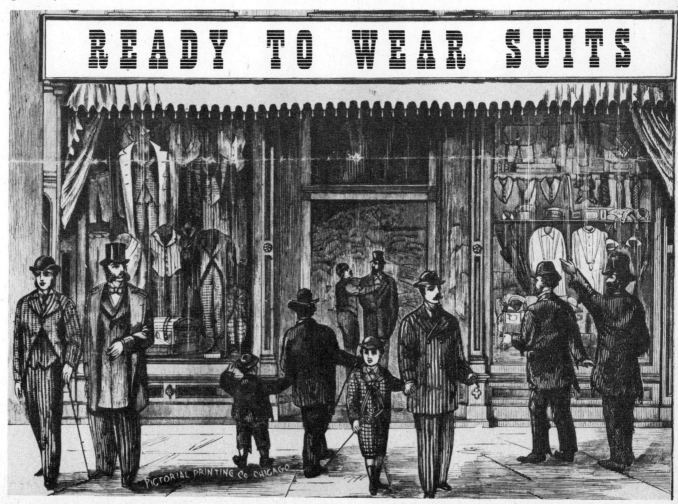

The manufacturers of shoes also made gigantic steps through the agency of the sewing machine, in combination with mass production, and the large market provided by the war. The infantry, which made up the mass of both armies, when not waiting for reinforcements or fighting a battle did little

Standard Screw Fastened Boots and Shoes.

but march, and march, and march. The McKay stitcher, coming at the psychological moment, convinced the soldiers that machines could produce shoes of superior quality and satisfactory appearance. Backed by the soldiers' preference, the machine-made shoes swept the market, and the old-time shoemaker was wise enough to hang up his leather apron and go to work in a shoe factory.

Government issue brought another change in men's attire by requiring underwear as an official part of the uniform. Most of the soldiers had never worn any underwear at all, but in the Army it was a must. After the war the knitting business began to thrive mightily, and this picture shows what the well-dressed man was wearing underneath.

When after the War of 1812 a movement was being organized to encourage American manufacture, the British began a campaign of dumping during which they unloaded enough plows in this country to glut the market for a decade, which was just what they wanted. They dumped other goods on a similar scale, but one article that they failed to dump was the washing machine. At the time there was no satisfactory washing machine, and American inventors very gallantly set out to produce one. During the next forty years they offered to the public no less than a dozen new models a year. Every man of ingenuity seemed determined to see to it that his wife was relieved of the burden of doing the family washing—by hand. In applications to the government for patents the washing machine was notorious—topping even that haven of the insane called the perpetual motion machine.

Applications for patents of all kinds declined during the Civil War, but in the last six months of 1868 no less than fifty patents for washing machines were applied for—and granted.

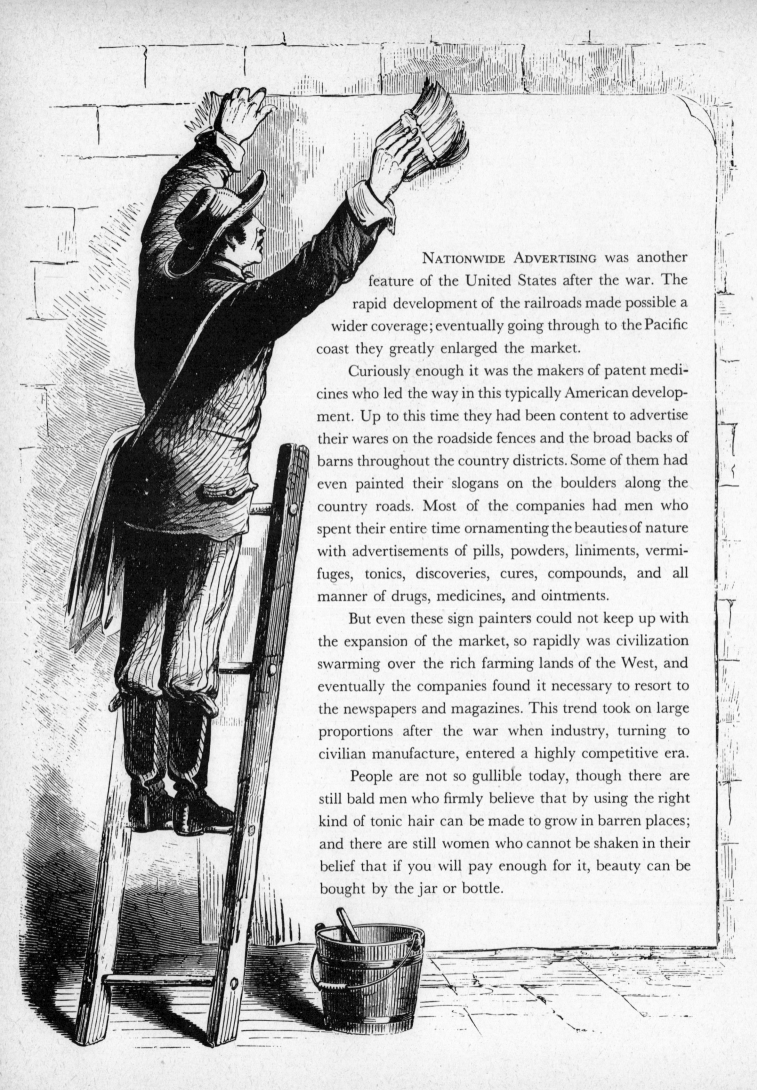

NATIONWIDE ADVERTISING was another feature of the United States after the war. The rapid development of the railroads made possible a wider coverage; eventually going through to the Pacific coast they greatly enlarged the market.

Curiously enough it was the makers of patent medicines who led the way in this typically American development. Up to this time they had been content to advertise their wares on the roadside fences and the broad backs of barns throughout the country districts. Some of them had even painted their slogans on the boulders along the country roads. Most of the companies had men who spent their entire time ornamenting the beauties of nature with advertisements of pills, powders, liniments, vermifuges, tonics, discoveries, cures, compounds, and all manner of drugs, medicines, and ointments.

But even these sign painters could not keep up with the expansion of the market, so rapidly was civilization swarming over the rich farming lands of the West, and eventually the companies found it necessary to resort to the newspapers and magazines. This trend took on large proportions after the war when industry, turning to civilian manufacture, entered a highly competitive era.

People are not so gullible today, though there are still bald men who firmly believe that by using the right kind of tonic hair can be made to grow in barren places; and there are still women who cannot be shaken in their belief that if you will pay enough for it, beauty can be bought by the jar or bottle.

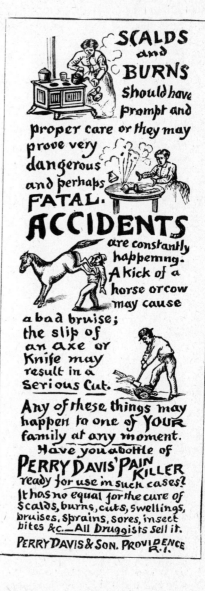
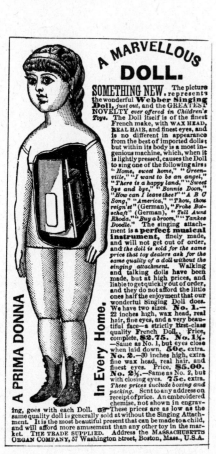

STOCK GAMBLING IN NEW YORK AT THE HEIGHT OF WAR PROSPERITY

Prosperity based on the business side of war is a delusion and a snare. It is a false prosperity based on destruction. No wealth has been produced. Ships are built only to be sunk. Ammunition has been made in gargantuan quantities only to be shot off. Old cities are destroyed, but no new cities are built, or if they are they soon become ghost cities. Houses are burned down for no good reason except that they belong to somebody on the other side, or perhaps somebody who only sympathizes with the other side. In the end they will have to pay the score. If you crush the other side, he can't pay; and if he crushes you—most certainly you aren't any better off than you were before. Indemnity may be punitive, but it never is remunerative.

At the end of the war the North was riding high. The South was ruined, but that was just incidental, though it was too bad. They shouldn't have started anything they couldn't finish. Business in the North was booming. Industrialization was flourishing. Rapid development of the West was opening a whole empire of new markets. It was a flush time. Every man was a king or a millionaire, or soon would be. But the wave of inflation reached its limits and began to ebb. The seventies brought corruption on a colossal scale. Confidence waned, and soon the country was in the grip of a panic.

In 1873 the collapse of the great banking house of Jay Cooke brought the country to the verge of ruin. Overexpansion was causing a severe attack of growing pains. The land itself was the only thing that seemed secure, and that was mortgaged to the limit. The development of the West came to a bitter, though temporary, halt. Many of the settlers did not even wait to have their mortgages foreclosed. They just walked out and went away to try a new start somewhere else.

Nobody thought in 1873 that the country would be cheerfully celebrating its centennial three years later. But that is the way with democracy—it has a quick comeback.

HARD TIMES—MORTGAGING THE OLD HOMESTEAD

LURE OF THE CITY

The crisis of the countryside accelerated another great migration: from country to city—from farm to factory. The cities now became the vast centers of industrialization, and they attracted the youth of the land as a magnet draws in the near-by filings.

Throughout the East, where the greatest industrial development was centered, only the dullards remained on the farms. The boys with brains and ambition wanted to go off to college and then settle in the cities and get a job and amount to something. Gradually the girls caught the idea. If they stayed behind, all they would get was the leavings. And what smart, bright, ambitious girl was ever satisfied to put up with leftovers, especially in the matter of suitors, biology, homemaking, and providing the world with the next generation?

The country press and pulpit denounced the city as a den of iniquity and a hotbed of vice and wickedness. They warned the new generation in a voice of thunder that they were hell-bent and on the brink of destruction. Of course this made it seem all the more attractive and romantic to the country youth bored to death with the farm and ripe for anything that promised to furnish an interesting adventure.

Street Life and Business

The attempt, usually futile, to describe New York was as much a challenge to the nineteenth century as the Grand Canyon presented to the twentieth. All agreed that the city was sinful, but nobody ever denied that it was the home of opportunity and a wonderful place to have a good time. Here youth and beauty were to be seen, a little judicious flirting—and perhaps some that was not so judicious. The young man-about-town was not at all backward about sizing up the passing pulchritude.

On every hand the new economic forces were making themselves felt—the vast accumulations of wealth, the business and financial structure, the concentration of railroads, the magnificent port into which the ships of all nations were constantly streaming to fetch and carry cargoes of vast importance in the business of the world. It was inevitable that this city should become a great center of intellectual progress, of social and artistic advancement, as well as the financial capital of a young and vigorous country just then coming of age as a world power. Merely to dwell in the midst of great affairs is a stimulating source of the discontent from which springs progress, and today we do not find it strange that it proved so strong an attraction for the youth of the land.

With due regard for other American cities no less important—Philadelphia, Boston, Chicago and the rest—the following pages will be devoted largely to New York. Here the forces of the new period were most tellingly observed and recorded by the writers and artists of the time. The migration, however, was general. There was no part of the country which did not feel it going or coming.

The innumerable visitors to New York—indeed to any large city—were agreed on one point: the most conspicuous element of city life was speed—with noise as a close second—and after that smell. A commentator of the time wrote, "In the streets all is hurry and bustle; the very carts, instead of being drawn by horses at a walking pace, are often met at a gallop, with

the carter standing in the front and driving by reins.

"The whole population seen in the streets seem to enjoy this bustle and add to it by their own rapid pace, as if they were all going to some place of appointment and were hurrying on under the apprehension of being too late."

UPPER FIFTH AVENUE—
A STUDY IN CONTRASTS

Strangers coming to New York were also struck with the fact that there were but two classes in the city—the poor and the rich. The middle class, the commentator adds, so numerous in other cities, hardly exists here at all. New York, it was said, resembles a lady with diamonds around her neck and the toes sticking out of her ragged shoes. Living in the city was so expensive that persons of moderate means were compelled to reside in the suburbs.

An endless crowd was pouring into the city between the hours of seven and nine in the morning to go to business and literally pouring out again between four and seven in the evening. In fair weather, it is explained, the inconvenience of such a life is trifling, but in the winter it is fearful, with the railroad tracks frequently obstructed by snowbanks and the outside dwellers either unable to reach the city or unwilling to risk spending a night in the cars stuck at some inaccessible point along the way. The cartoonist found the commuter's life a fertile field for jests.

MR. NOSEGAY RESIDES IN THE SUBURBS. HE IS LATE THIS MORNING AND MRS. N. INFORMS HIM THAT SHE HEARS THE TRAIN IN THE DISTANCE.

MR. NOSEGAY RUSHES FOR THE TRAIN, THE DOGS OF THE VILLAGE ACCOMPANY HIM.

A NARROW ESCAPE, IN WHICH HE RECEIVES SOME BRUISES AND LOSES HIS HAT AND BASKET.

How to Get Across Broadway was one of the serious problems of New Yorkers of the seventies. The traffic was as dense as today, with the clattering of hoofs, the rattling of iron tires on the stone-paved roadway, and the shouting of the drivers making up what was well described as the "roar of traffic." There were not in those days any traffic controls except the occasional policeman who would stop the traffic and allow a group of children to scurry across.

SINGULARLY STUDIOUS APPEARANCE
OF GENTLEMEN IN A STREET CAR

The transit problem was as acute after the Civil War as it is today. More persons were usually standing than sitting in both the horse-drawn street cars and the overcrowded stages. Fares leaped on and off the slowly moving horsecars without waiting for them to stop. In the stages if you desired change your money was handed up to the driver through a hole near his feet. The change came back in a small envelope supposed to have been sealed at the office to prevent pilfering by the driver. All too often the change was incorrect and the passenger found little advantage in arguing with the driver's feet through a six-inch hole that could be closed with a slam by the driver.

"PLENTY OF ROOM," SHOUTS THE CONDUCTOR

THE FIRST TRAIN ON THE GILBERT ELEVATED RAILROAD PASSING THROUGH SIXTH AVENUE, NEAR THE JEFFERSON MARKET POLICE COURT, APRIL 29, 1878

The elevated railway shown here passing Jefferson Market offered some relief to the overcrowding, but the idea was not accepted without a fight. Owners of surface transportation lines as well as property owners took the matter to court. The "el" went through in spite of all claims that the noise would ruin business and the unsightly structure would permanently disfigure the "natural beauty" of the city. The clergy, too, raised their voices in protest, predicting that the thunder of the passing trains would put an end to all public worship. It was in response to this complaint that *Puck* suggested a solution which, curiously enough, shows the preacher at the wrong end of the amplifier.

SHOE-LACE MAN

THE SPECTACLE WOMAN

UMBRELLA DEALER

DO YOU LOVE YOUR BABY?

GET YOUR RAZORS GROUND!

MUSTACHE SELLER

SORTING EGGS

The great American dream of unlimited opportunity was in full swing as far back as the forties. The newsboy, the shoestring seller, the most humble street vendor was well aware of the fact that if he worked hard, attended to business, and took advantage of his opportunities there was no reason why he should not make good. A high station in life was not at all impossible simply because he was starting from the bottom.

The Horatio Alger stories are quite in keeping with the trend of the time. They express the universal belief that starting at the bottom of the ladder is by no means an impediment to success but is rather a period of necessary training not unlike the finger exercises which are supposed to bring mastery of the keys to the fine musician. These books, however, introduce another ingredient which must be added to thrift and industry. They introduce the moral element—to be successful you must be good.

The Newsboys were the most energetic among child vendors. Many a successful businessman got his start by peddling papers. Those young salesmen rushed "hither and thither with their arms full of wisdom." One visitor observed that they were almost as characteristic of New York as were the dogs of Constantinople. Their agressive sales policy helped to keep many a slum family from starving.

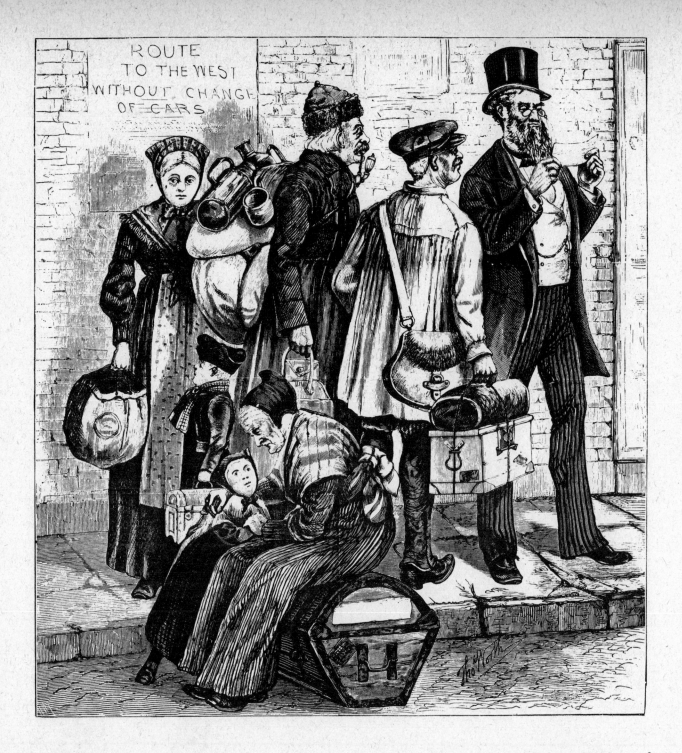

EMIGRANTS ASKING THEIR WAY added much color to the city streets. Before the days of Ellis Island it was at Castle Garden that the immigrants landing at New York were received. Castle Garden was at the virtual tip of Manhattan Island beside the Battery. Here a never-ending stream of newcomers arrived in this country of opportunity, for the American magnet was not long in making itself felt in all the European countries. Germans landed here on their way to Wisconsin and Illinois, Swedes and Norwegians en route to Minnesota and the Dakotas, Poles for the coal mines of Pennsylvania and West Virginia, and Irish who, though they may have been intending to go on to go farther inland, almost invariably settled in New York. American industry, which had by the fifties outgrown the American labor market, combined and sent agents to Europe to stimulate emigration. The cheapness of transatlantic travel when steerage passage across the ocean could be had for ten dollars sped the travelers on their way to the new world.

To the Irish fell a great part of the tasks involving unskilled labor. They dug the ditches and laid the pavements; they graded the railroads and excavated the canals; they ripped up the pavements and laid the street railways; they dug the cellars and laid up the walls for the new buildings. They lived in the filthy and overcrowded tenement districts and slums. They carried the hods, they swung the picks, they plied the shovels, and all for starvation wages. A man started in at a dollar a day and was usually a long time working himself up to two dollars a day, which for a long time was tops. They went to work on a seven o'clock whistle, and nobody ever knocked off until six. Many of the better jobs, such as driving the stages and horsecars, being easier work, required longer hours, never less than twelve and often as much as sixteen hours, and all for two dollars a day. In domestic service a good maid might get as much as two dollars and a half a week, but the average was anywhere from one dollar and a half to two dollars—with plenty of applicants looking for jobs.

THE STREET-SWEEPERS ANSWERING TO THE INSPECTOR'S ROLL-CALL

NEW MARKETS were created by the rapid growth of the urban population. Bazaars, dry goods, and variety stores sprang up all over the city—catering to the tastes and pocketbooks of the various neighborhoods. The shop windows began to fill up with goods on display, and the great national pastime of window shopping came into existence. The love of better things and more expensive things was encouraged in every way—as if such a thing ever needed much encouragement.

But new methods of merchandising were also being contrived, and experiments were being conducted on the principle of quick sales and small profits, the natural outgrowth of the cheap and rapid machine production. The time had not yet come for Mr. Woolworth to launch his thriving bazaars with the red front and gold lettering. The prices had come no lower than twenty and twenty-five cents by the end of the sixties, but the five-and-ten was just around the corner, though nobody seemed to know it.

The store windows of Broadway and West Twenty-third Street, as well as the entire Madison Square neighborhood, were filled with luxury items to tempt a queen.

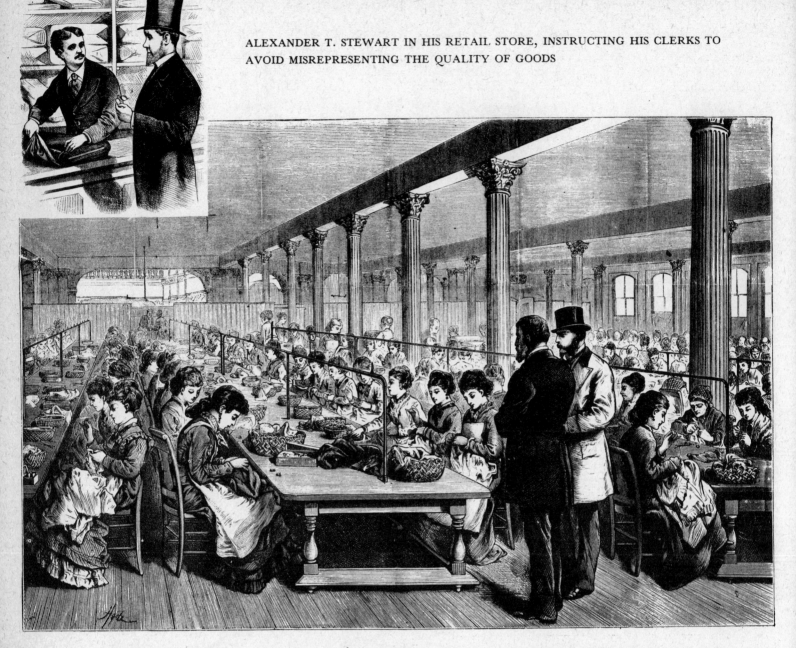

ALEXANDER T. STEWART IN HIS RETAIL STORE, INSTRUCTING HIS CLERKS TO AVOID MISREPRESENTING THE QUALITY OF GOODS

THE SEWING ROOM AT A. T. STEWART'S, BETWEEN NINTH AND TENTH STREETS, BROADWAY AND FOURTH AVENUE

Another very definite change in merchandising policy took place in the seventies when an Irish immigrant named A. T. Stewart revised the old-time bargaining method of retailing by introducing a fixed price which was plainly marked on each article offered for sale. Prospective shoppers had chuckled over the announcements made in the papers, but when they started their usual tactics of trying to beat down the price they learned to their astonishment that the announcements meant just what they had said. There was some grumbling and some threatening to take business elsewhere, but the idea caught on. The store was a success, but Mr. Stewart was much criticized for his dictatorial attitude toward his employees. His store was organized on the mass-production basis with girls working in his sewing room from seven-thirty in the morning until nine or ten at night, many of them paid as little as five dollars a week.

DANIEL DREW SELLING FIFTY
THOUSAND SHARES OF ERIE
STOCK AT "FIFTY-FIVE,"
SELLER'S OPTION, ONE YEAR.

With so much easy money floating around it was inevitable that some error should creep in. The error came from the operations of manipulators who found it impossible to keep from rigging the market with reckless self-interest, thinking nothing of ruining the business and the fortunes of thousands of innocent investors. At first these operators were for the most part lone wolves, robbing each other whenever opportunity arose. One of the first great market struggles came in the fight for personal supremacy—perhaps survival—between Commodore Vanderbilt and Daniel Drew. The Commodore had made his start in life with a small ferryboat plying between New York and Staten Island. Drew was a cattle man. Vanderbilt was a bull, Drew a bear. For years the two jockeyed with the market, each trying his best to ruin the other. Indeed they were so engaged with their personal war of extinction that they did not realize that they had a common enemy until a young man named Jay Gould came down from upstate and beat them both to the draw.

Probably no single invention did more for the unification of our sprawling economy than the telegraph. We were indeed a country of magnificent distances greatly in need of methods of communication which were faster than the proverbial man on horseback. With the coming of the telegraph Big Business greatly extended its power. The quickness in making decisions—or changing them—multiplied the evils of the great corporations and combinations, one of the biggest grabs being the taking over of the streets by the powerful wire companies. Monopolies and rings were thriving and reaching out in all directions.

SPECULATION, stepson of business, had come to America with the earliest settlers. George Washington himself, a wildcat speculator in real estate, liked to put a bet on the races and notes in one of his diaries the money he lost on a cockfight. The inability to refuse a wager was in the American blood. Easy come, easy go. I'll bet my house will burn down. How much will you bet? Insurance.

Men with money flocked naturally together backing railroads, steamship lines, banks, and other joint ventures. Manipulators with millions to risk came drifting in from outlying districts. They went about the destruction of their enemies and competitors with little thought for the innocent investors who were left holding the sack.

The entire economy of the nation was as tangled as the wires on Broadway. Without adequate regulation the trusts and combinations had things their own way. Between overexpansion on the one hand and lack of confidence on the other, the nation found itself faced with a strange convulsion of the stock market which developed into a crash known as the "Panic of Seventy-three." It was a nationwide collapse which spared no group or class from the ravages of the calamity.

When the centennial year of 1876 was approaching, nothing definite had happened to change the financial situation. No reforms had been enacted. No economic salvation had been worked out. But the people had become thoroughly bored with the depression and wanted to have some fun. They accordingly threw themselves into the Centennial Celebration with fine spirit and produced the first of our great national fairs.

PHILADELPHIA CENTENNIAL UNDER CONSTRUCTION: PLACING COLOSSAL STATUES AT THE BASE OF
THE DOME OF MEMORIAL HALL

GRAND ENTRANCE TO HORTICULTURAL HALL

Interlude: The Centennial

The Centennial was the first great landmark of American growth. Here the youthful nation stopped and took account of itself. It surveyed its physical development and laid out for all to see its mechanical and technological advances. It showed a growing appreciation of the arts and crafts as well as architecture and the design and building of furniture suited to our own peculiar needs. For almost a generation the country had been so absorbed in its own destiny that it had taken little interest in developments abroad, and it found the displays of foreign countries stimulating in the extreme, furnishing as they did the opportunity for comparison. Balanced as the country was between possible disaster and the prospects of a vast national prosperity, people put aside their fears and streamed into Philadelphia as if the answer to their problems was to be found by a treasure hunt among the exhibits.

THE CORLISS BEVEL-GEAR-CUTTING MACHINE

In Machinery Hall people stood goggle-eyed before the mechanical lathes and gear-cutting machines as they watched articles automatically shaping into forms which had hitherto been made only by human hands.

Visitors who had never seen any machine larger than a corn sheller or possibly a buzz saw looked aghast at the big Corliss Steam Engine, and when the wheels began to move as President Grant and Emperor Dom Pedro opened the throttle they felt that they had indeed witnessed the wonder of the age.

THE TORCH OF LIBERTY WAS CLIMBED BY THOUSANDS OF VISITORS

And as for air-conditioning devices—they often created too much of a blow for the unwary visitors.

DOM PEDRO AND DR. BELL AT THE CENTENNIAL

It was at the Centennial that Professor Alexander Graham Bell first exhibited in a big way his recent invention of a little gadget he called the telephone. People glanced at it as they passed, but since there were no wheels going around and no machinery to watch, the public took little interest in it. They were far more interested in a huge plow exhibited by Daniel Webster and paid much more attention to a whistle made from a pig's tail. Some of the books written about the Centennial failed to mention the telephone, so little was the importance attached to a machine that would do nothing but carry the human voice. And when Bell tried to sell stock in his company he could find nobody in the whole of Boston willing to invest any money in it.

Another exhibit at Philadelphia which aroused little attention was the electric light. People chuckled over it. Funny way to make light, better give them a good old kerosene lamp. People passed by without noticing an electric motor which was driving a small pump. A thousand dollars invested here might have made a man a millionaire. But who was there that had any use for a pump driven by an electric motor?

NEW YEAR'S GREETINGS BY TELEPHONE, 1882

THE TYPEWRITER, too, was almost completely ignored. The idea was regarded as ingenious, but why should anybody want to write by machinery when it could be done so much better and faster by hand? There was a question of etiquette, too. Nothing, of course, but the crudest sort of business letter could conceivably be written by machine. That's what they thought. Few fancied that this machine would open up a new world for the women: With the improvement of the typewriter and its adoption into the business offices its operation was taken over almost entirely by the female stenographer.

In spite of its vast size and its determination to be up-to-date, the Centennial was not without the flavor of an overdressed county fair. There were no ox-pulling and no plowing contests, but the occasion was not allowed to pass without the crowning of a Queen of Love and Beauty.

The hot sausages came to us minus their German name, and the tournament, said to be the Southern National Game, is supposed to appeal to a nostalgic sense of chivalry still surviving in the South.

CHINESE PORCELAIN DEALERS, English furniture makers, engineers from Germany, reindeer hunters from Lapland—made the Centennial an exciting event. It has been said that this exhibit marks the turning point in American taste and affords the first sign of relief from the red-plush stuffiness of the Victorian period. It was a faint sign yet, but the "Fair" conditioned the public for better things to come. Few Americans were at this time widely traveled, and here they found the beautiful and curious things of the world brought to their own front door for their inspection.

The Last Load
Can't you take a few things more.

Private Lives

The Centennial acquainted the American people with a wealth of household utensils and devices designed to make life easier. The real problem of the city dweller, however, was not quite solved at Philadelphia. There was the question of just how long he would have a home to live in. He had always to be ready to move. The housing shortage, especially in New York, was acute. Even after the building of the first apartment houses, which began to appear in 1870, it was freely said around the city that to be sure of a home a family must have a place of its own.

As business establishments multiplied in the downtown districts, the residence portion of the city went farther and farther uptown. But for all the building of houses and apartments the population is usually greater than the housing facilities, and many householders preferred to board—an old New York custom. As far back as the eighteen thirties the city was called "one great boarding house."

The shortage of houses was, on a smaller scale of course, as bad as today; and the constantly advancing rents, on which there were no controls, kept the householders shifting from year to year. Long leases were hard to get, and the constant change of leaseholds was expensive and vexatious. It seems like an old story to us today; but that's the way life is—the same thing over and over again.

If the middle-class family was uncomfortable in its overcrowded flats and boarding houses, the slum dwellers were even more uncomfortable in their miserable hovels and their cold-water walk-ups. The slum district around the Five Points was described as exceeding in degradation, criminality, and horror any like area in the entire world. Doubtless this was overdrawn, for the slum areas of London have been famous for centuries, and even they were beauty spots compared with the slums in the cities of the eastern Mediterranean district.

A LANDLORD'S SKETCH

A TENANT'S SKETCH

AN IMPATIENT DINNER PARTY AWAITING THE RETURN OF GASLIGHT

There was no lack of living space among those of the upper crust; palatial mansions of the Dollar Nobility had begun to appear even before the Civil War. New York abounded with houses especially designed for the goingon of high society during the days of the bustle and the stuffed shirt. These homes of the rich did lead the way in raising the living standards—with the first bathrooms, gaslights, and other contraptions then imperfect with their newness, but since outmoded, discarded, or improved beyond recognition.

THE MANSION OF A. T. STEWART on the corner of Fifth Avenue and Thirty-Fourth Street was the most luxurious of all the fabulous palaces of the period. The first two floors were built of Carrara marble with ceilings over eighteen feet in height. The entire interior was built of imported materials—the marble staircase, the rosewood and gilt onyx-topped furniture, the crimson plush hangings. Even the artist who painted the murals on the walls was imported, an Italian who had his day but whose name has gone to oblivion along with the murals which were destroyed when the house was torn down to make way for a department store. There was a presidential suite in the house, called in its time General Grant's room. It contained what was said to be the first pair of twin beds in this country, both of them full size. Cunningly concealed lavatory apparatus were praised as a new height in domestic engineering.

It was a period not only of great ostentation but of great activity on the part of the social climber who hoped to gain entrance into the so-called "old society" by making a big splurge with his newly acquired riches. The art and treasure of all corners of the world were used to decorate the parlors of men who had made fortunes in soap, steel rails, whisky, overalls; and the miracle of it was that so many of them succeeded in getting into society. It was curious to find the armor of medieval knights standing in the hallway of a captain of industry whose boldest stroke, as Beard puts it, was a courageous guess on the stock market.

BOUDOIR—RESIDENCE OF W. H. DEFOREST, ESQ.

Emulation of the lucky rich being such as it is, the craze for the collection of art treasures, doodads, and brick-a-brack was taken up by the middle classes, turning their parlors into what was described as museums of esthetic horrors, "mortuary chapels for the reception of guests." The Victorians made little provision in their homes for the comfortable incidentals of living. However, they seldom failed to take care of the eventuality of death, providing a niche at the turn of the stairway to permit the passing of a coffin. Mrs. Spofford, the unchallenged arbiter in matters of home decoration, proclaimed: "Provided that there is room enough to move about without walking over the furniture, there is hardly likely to be too much in a room."

The home and children were the woman's domain, and men made little effort to change the status quo. On the wife and the mother rested the chief responsibility for connubial bliss. While the Civil War had extended the aura of respectability into the office and had enlisted what was proving to be an ever-increasing army of working girls, women of leisure took up embroidery, painting on glass or china, lacemaking, and even waxwork. Anything, or so it seems, to keep them in the house. The established female decorum was a hard thing to beat. The intellectual progress of woman was hampered, but not suppressed, though as usual the higher the social stratum, the greater the independence.

THE CHILDREN'S HOUR—
TELLING FAIRY STORIES

NEW ENGLAND MAIDEN'S BEST FRIEND—PATENT ATTACHMENT FOR BOOKREST

There was increasing dissatisfaction even among the kitchen drudges. They began to long for a sufficient degree of education to enable them to get into a nice clean office, where they would be troubled no more with dishpan hands and housemaid's knee. Enough of them were successful to aggravate that great unsolved American problem: The Servant Question.

Earlier in the American scene domestic employment had existed on a rather democratic basis, with the menial status softened or even belied by the use of the term "help" instead of "servant" or "maid" or "cook" or even "hired girl." This was especially true in the rural districts where the kitchen worker was often the daughter of some neighboring farmer. In such case the girl was allowed to eat with the family, getting up to wait on the table as occasion demanded. She was also permitted to sit with the family during her spare time and to participate in the family prayers.

To meet the shortage a great mass of Irish and German girls were imported, and while they peopled the kitchens of the cities and occasionally the country, they knew little of the American way of life and had to learn their new jobs from the ground up. Their stubborn and ignorant ways often tried the patience of their mistresses and put a very definite end to the use of the word "help" for kitchen workers.

MISTRESS AND MAID

MISTRESS. "Fix the fire."

MISTRESS. "Excuse me, Bridget, for troubling you, but any time when convenient—would you please—if not *too* much trouble—just fix this fire a little—please?"

MISTRESS. "Bridget dear, is it quite warm enough for you? Don't you think I had better fix the fire a little?"

Schools of Cookery began to blossom along in the seventies. Since cooks were hard to get, the ladies had to learn how to cook for themselves. The first of these schools was opened in New York in 1874, followed by the opening of the Boston Cooking School three years later. Here, to popularize the institution the students were permitted to serve gentlemen guests.

America has long been the most abundantly fed nation in the world. Whether or not it is the best fed is a matter of opinion. Mrs. Trollope, writing back in the eighteen thirties, noted our consumption of an extraordinary quantity of bacon. She noticed that ham and beefsteaks appeared morning, noon, and night and complained of the strange incongruity with which we mix things together. Our bread, she admits, is everywhere excellent. The only trouble is that nobody eats it, preferring half-baked hot rolls both morning and evening.

It is no doubt true that until the introduction of oatmeal and some of the other cereal preparations, America did eat a pretty hearty breakfast. Fruit and coffee with some kind of bread, toast, or rolls was almost universal, and in addition one had the choice of steak or chops, or possibly ham and eggs with a generous portion of fried potatoes. Then for dessert came a stack of buckwheat cakes and maple syrup or perhaps a large segment of pie. In Boston, pie for breakfast was long a persistent custom, along with a big plate of pork and beans, especially on Sunday morning when one had to be well fortified to endure a sermon which was likely to drone on for a good hour and a half.

Food was cheap in the old days. Good beef could be had for eight to ten cents a pound, and the best cuts from sixteen to twenty-four cents a pound. There was, we are told, always an abundance of venison, and day laborers working for six to ten dollars a week were able to keep a large family from starving. The canning of fish and vegetables was just beginning, and even the milk was put up in this convenient form. Rationing, of course, had not been dreamed of. And some families said grace both before and after meals . . . and no wonder.

There can be little doubt that America has become vastly more food-conscious than it was a generation or two ago. The culinary standards have risen steadily along with the prices.

EATING PLACES FOR THE WHITE-COLLAR WORKER and the employee without the lunch pail were springing up all over the city wherever there were people to patronize them. These places were and are strictly American in flavor. In Europe and the older countries people are accustomed to spend more time over their meals. They eat slowly, they talk, they make more of a social occasion over a chunk of bread and a slab of cheese than we do over a full-course dinner. Our speed and devotion to the task at hand are often interpreted as rudeness when it is really no more than haste to be done with eating and let some other hungry fellow take our place.

Burne-Jones, the English painter, while on a visit to America, remarked that the words "quick lunch" gave him indigestion. It was probably nothing but the food. We are a young nation and full of ambition, and we can think of more interesting things to do than watching a companion slowly move his chin up and down while we slowly do the same thing. Dining, like contemplation, is something which takes time. But if a quick lunch isn't quick—what good is it?

THE RESTAURANTS OF NEW YORK were a true mirror of the city's classes. Eating places ranged from the humble "one-penny" restaurant to the fashionable hotels on Fifth Avenue where tycoons outdid each other with streams of champagn and culinary extravagances. At one function, the cigarettes were wrapped in hundred-dollar bills; at another, fine black pearls were given to the diners in their oysters.

And there was a similar variety as far as table habits were concerned. Visiting Englishmen of the last century, always generous in their outpour of criticism, found grace quite lacking in American eating habits. T. C. Grattan, an Englishman traveling in America, wrote, "Eating with the knife, loading the plate with numerous incongruous kinds of food, abruptness of demeanour are the common habits of the table d'hote." Reports such as these prompted Fanny Ellsler to equip herself with a dozen or so napkins before embarking for America. They also made the populace responsive to etiquette books of the period. Our illustration does not seem to neglect a single pitfall, and Emily Post's forerunner used the force of visualization to make the message stick.

BAD MANNERS AT THE TABLE.

No. 1. Tips back his chair.
" 2. Eats with his mouth too full.
" 3. Feeds a dog at the table.
" 4. Holds his knife improperly.
" 5. Engages in violent argument at the meal-time.
" 6. Lounges upon the table.
" 7. Brings a cross child to the table.

No. 8. Drinks from the saucer, and laps with his tongue the last drop from the plate.
" 9. Comes to the table in his shirt-sleeves, and puts his feet beside his chair.
" 10. Picks his teeth with his fingers.
" 11. Scratches her head and is frequently unnecessarily getting up from the table.

LUNCHEON AT DELMONICO'S

With its fine hotels manned by famous chefs from all over the world, gourmets have sought to give America a new sense of the culinary arts. In addition to giving themselves dyspepsia and stomach ulcers they have given the world a very comprehensive idea of where to get the finest food in the land. The American bill of fare is noted all over the world for its abundance. Its length, size, and the multiplicity of items is often baffling to the diner. And added to this the foreign languages which some of the restaurateurs affect would be enough to drive diners away if they were not intrigued by the sound or the looks of the names of some of the dishes listed. Delmonico's, perhaps the most noted of the Victorian eating places in New York, was as proud of its clientele as of its menu and strove to keep out objectionable characters regardless of their wealth or prominence. The establishment maintained a black list on which it placed the name of any person who raised a disturbance or in any way annoyed the guests. Persons on the black list were permitted to enter the place. Indeed they could not legally be stopped. They were allowed to seat themselves at table and to order. But the orders never were filled. At least that's the way the story goes. There is probably a moral here somewhere, and wouldbe diners who sit too long without being served might do well to look into their past.

The hotels were early pioneers in inside plumbing. They had bathrooms of a sort, though many of the smaller and older ones still depended on the old reliable washbowl and pitcher to keep the customer clean.

The city at large had suffered from "water troubles" since its very inception. The wells were steadily deteriorating. With the increase of population the water level was rapidly falling, and with the seepage of salt water brought in by the pressure from outside the island the quality of such well water as was to be had became almost undrinkable.

TEA WATER DELIVERED AT THE DOOR

PUBLIC WELLS were maintained by the city at various points, but these, too, were becoming brackish, and the companies which brought in and sold water by the gallon from the outside were doing a tremendous business. The wagons of the water seller were as numerous as the sprinkling carts of a later day. Then came the typhoid fever. They did not call it by that name, but it had all the symptoms.

It was not until 1862 that the Croton reservoir was finished and ready for business; and then only a small part of the city was furnished with water mains. The existence of the reservoir did not insure the supply of clean water. Apostles of cleanliness often found themselves served with chowder in their bathroom tub.

Interior plumbing was regarded at first not only as unhealthful, but as immoral, and local boards of health considered using the crude equipment of the day only under the care of the family doctor. But the motion was lost.

[132]

A MINING BATHHOUSE AT LEAD-
VILLE, COLORADO

The domestic bathroom was frequently not even a room. It was a corner in the barn with a tub informally rigged up and the hot water supplied via teakettle. Hailed as a big step forward was a closet with a tiny washbowl fed by quarter-inch pipes and toilet arrangements tucked into a dark corner. Sometimes the equipment was hidden behind a curtain at the end of a hallway. Sewer gas was all over the house, but the health authorities soon straightened that out by requiring a water-locked trap. After this the plumbing fixtures began to improve. Investors got busy suggesting all kinds of shower gadgets. Simple necessity gave way to good taste and eventually approached the elegant. The zinc lining disappeared from the cabinet bathtubs and was replaced with white enamel and eventually porcelain. Fixtures came out of the closets and were given a room by themselves. Water mains were extended until at last they served every quarter of the city. Today a hotel room without a bath or shower is something to apologize for.

COMBINED MORNING
WORKOUT AND SHOWER-
BATH

HOTEL BATHROOM, 1880

While technology and invention had made life easier, it had not as yet brought into production machinery to solve the social problems of life in a crowded city, especially for children. Bicycles had not yet become a popular reality. Roller skates were not far off, though smooth pavements on which to use them had not yet come and they were practical only in the skating rink. And then, as now, to give the baby an airing somebody must do a deal of perambulating. There was still some reasonably fresh air in Central Park if one could only get the children there—and teach them to keep off the grass. Going fishing, climbing trees, or taking a ride on top of a hayload were pastimes for the country child. In the city, however, a children's party back in the sixties could really become a function.

According to a contemporary journal, at a party given in Brooklyn for a lady of eleven years, the hair dressed in the latest style was frizzed, puffed, powdered, and adorned with flowers. Four-button white kid gloves were worn; while French kid boots, matching the dresses in color, encased the feet. A little girl of seven was dressed in rose-colored silk trimmed with point-appliqué flounces and covered with gold and gems. The cost of this outfit was estimated at seven thousand dollars. Children were not children yet but grownups in miniature.

BOY'S OUTFIT 1878

Just as it is difficult to teach an old dog new tricks, it was practically impossible to dislodge Victorian parents from their preconceived notions as to the upbringing of children. So long as family life was lived in the country there was plenty of outlet for the animal spirits of the young, but confined in the city apartment with little opportunity to blow off steam, it was inevitable that they should get out of hand. The shyness of the country child had long been proverbial; with animals he was quite at home, but with people he

SNOWBALL PARTY IN THE PARLOR

was bashful and ill at ease. With city children it was the other way around, and they were not long in winning for themselves the reputation of being pert and disrespectful. This was especially noticeable to foreigners, who considered them spoiled beyond all redemption. This was in all probability the beginning of the overthrow of stiff-necked Victorian authority. Even American writers were not unaware of the filial irreverence of the period, and one cuttingly referred to the problem of children as being the "painless extinction of their elders."

It was, however, a time of scientific advancement, with great improvement in the feeding, care, and medication of the younger generation and real strides in the matter of preventive measures of dealing with disease.

THE SMALLPOX EXCITEMENT—DR. CHAMBON VACCINATING PATIENTS IN HIS PARLOR WITH VIRUS TAKEN DIRECTLY FROM THE ANIMAL

"DOESN'T HE THINK HE LOOKS NICE?"

A CALLER WHO CALLS TO FILL HIS STOMACH

THE NEW YEAR'S DAY CARD BASKET

In the Matter of Holidays the town was somewhat inclined to imitate the country. For Thanksgiving and Christmas the city family went back to the country if possible. Both were occasions for stuffing with good food, and persons with a country background instinctively thought of the early days on the farm—with the appetite keen and the digestion unimpaired by highly-seasoned food hastily bolted down. If the farm was still in the hands of the old folks or some other member of the family, the annual peregrination was almost certain to occur, with the city visitors riding out to the farm from the nearest railroad station.

Other holidays, especially New Year's Day and Easter, were likely to be celebrated according to the customs of the city, each developing its own etiquette based predominantly on ostentation. Each became in its way a great fashion show. The custom of making New Year's calls, now happily or unhappily discontinued, was a typically Victorian event. The underlying idea was that everybody should call on everybody else to wish them a Happy New Year. The practice was, however, for the women to stay at home and the men to do all the calling. Clad in their voluminous Victorian fripperies and prettified within an inch of their lives, the ladies languished on their plush-covered furniture and waited for the men to drop in.

By leaving his card in a basket hung on a doorknob, the visitor could earn a credit for having paid his respects without taking the punishment of mingling with disagreeable people and then inventing an excuse to get away. And in addition to this there was a limit to the number of toasts a man could drink during visiting hours. The story is that the men would start with the more distant friends and work homeward, and that sometimes they made it.

Women vied with each other in the number of calls received, and the children were allowed to keep the score.

EASTER SUNDAY—CRACKING OF THE EASTER EGG, AND BUDDING FORTH OF THE SPRING FASHIONS, 1873

Easter, being primarily a church festival, was treated with less conviviality than the advent of the New Year. Instead of going from house to house to drink innumerable toasts, people went to church ostensibly to worship—but all too often to be seen in a new spring outfit and to see what others looked like in their spring outfits. Weather permitting, the Easter celebration is one of the most cheerful and colorful of the year.

Devotions are put aside as the church service ends, and with a precision that is almost automatic the Easter Parade forms itself all along Fifth Avenue. It's a harmless affair. Thousands walk the street and show off their new clothes, while other thousands look them over.

For the children colored eggs used to be hidden in the apartment. In Washington the old medieval custom of egg-rolling was revived by Dolly Madison in the first decade of the nineteenth century. Children competed in rolling their hard-boiled eggs down the terraces of the Capitol lawn. Later the frolic was transferred to the lawn of the White House grounds where it is still an annual event of great interest to children and photographers.

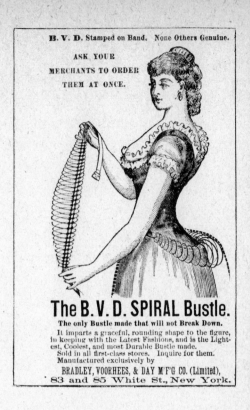
It was along in the eighties when the bustle was at its best in America. The hoop skirt had been all the rage throughout the Civil War period. For this we have to thank the beautiful Empress Eugénie. One glance at this exquisite being was enough to convince the feminine beholder that all she needed to make herself equally beautiful was a gown like that of the Empress. Originally made of crinoline, it was soon discovered that a better effect could be achieved by the use of whalebone or bamboo. And naturally it was only a short step from the hoop skirt to the bustle—a backward step perhaps. And it was here that Yankee ingenuity took a hand, inventing various types of bustle that would rise again after having been sat on. How well this bustle performed may be judged by the story of the Washington lady who walked to church and home again with a toy rooster perched on her bustle.

LADIES' DRESS-REFORM MEETING AT FREEMAN PLACE CHAPEL, BOSTON, MASS., 1874

Neither the bustle nor the hoop skirt aroused a great deal of admiration on the part of the men. Both contraptions were far from graceful. Both were extremely costly and easily damaged or disabled. It was, however, the women themselves who eventually went in for dress reform along more naturalistic lines. Frances Willard coined the phrase that niggardly waists and niggardly brains went together, and Elizabeth Stuart Phelps, who was rabidly opposed to the corset, went so far as to open a shop for the sale of "dress-reform garments." Physicians, who can usually be counted on to take sides in any sort of physiological discussion, declared that the injurious style of dress employed by women was doing as much to destroy the race "as is man by alcoholism." The race, however, is still with us, and only a glance at the magazines is required to show that the corset factories are thriving.

THIRTEEN INCHES FROM THE GROUND—ACME OF DARING

So far as the lady was concerned, there were no legs in the etiquette book of the nineteenth century. That there were limbs somewhere underneath the voluminous dresses was very faintly hinted at. To show an ankle in getting in or out of her carriage was almost a scandal. For a girl to cross her legs in company would have been indecent, and would have subjected the perpetrator of such outrage to the charge of being "common." Captain Marryat tells of finding the legs of a piano in a young ladies' seminary "fitted with modest little trousers." It was the stage which finally stripped the country of such false and silly modesty. Daring young girls who had nice legs insisted on showing them, though not without some protest from lady censors with a tape measure.

WOMAN'S CROWNING BEAUTY has come in for a lot of discussion for centuries—perhaps eons. The prehistoric man had a use for it; for in addition to braiding it into cord for his snares he used it as a means of helping her into his cave after he had succeeded in stealing her from some other prehistoric man. The idea that this peculiar material growing on her head could be used for beautifying her came a little later. But once it took hold it was never abandoned. Even the Seven Sutherland Sisters could not produce enough hair to satisfy the demands of the belle of the eighties. She must call on the horse, the sheep, the hemp, anything, in fact, to make it appear that she had a great deal more hair on her head than actually grew there. Again the ingenious Yankee came along with his stuffed wire forms. What these forms must have looked like after a man had yielded to an uncontrollable desire to pillow a lady's head in his lap can only be imagined.

"THE BURDENS OF FASHION."
WHAT WE *MUST* COME TO BEFORE LONG!

FLIRTATION

Relations between the sexes back in the seventies and eighties were not essentially different from the boy-girl situation today. Then as now the emotional attitude of the one toward the other was based on sex attraction.

No youth, however good his intentions, ever fell in love with a stick of wood. Moonlight was of course an indispensable adjunct of romance; it was so safe, and so cheap.

But a pretty nursemaid could manage to get along without moonlight—if she was pretty enough, and resourceful. It was the mating instinct which drew one person to another.

In the present days of frankness there is little excuse for a boy and girl to misunderstand each other. She knows what he's up to, and he knows how far she is willing to go. But in the Victorian courtship, surrounded as it was by obstacles, dampers, hindrances, and safeguards, there was every opportunity in the world for the young couple to misunderstand and misconstrue. A mere bit of amiability on the part of the girl might send the youth scurrying to her father for consent to pay court to the daughter. Propriety prevented his saying anything to the girl about it until he had obtained parental permission. And even after he had passed muster with the parents the girl might reject him with surprise and bewilderment.

If a man was every inch a gentleman, as it was presumed he would be, he did not attempt to fold a lady in his arms until the wedding night. On acceptance of his proposal he begged permission to seal the sacred promise with a chaste kiss—at least that is what the rules of etiquette called for. What instinct and mutual attraction may have been urging at that par-ticular moment could easily have been something quite different, human nature being such as it is. Underneath the ruffles and furbelows a very eager heart may have been beating, and when eager hearts begin to respond to each other the rule book might just as well be put back on the shelf.

The correct and the incorrect way of doing things were being constantly called to the attention of the Victorian youth. If they made mistakes, if they were on occasion indiscreet, it was not because of any lack of advice from their overstuffed elders.

Early life in America had indeed toned down the sartorial tastes of the young man of society. Living in the woods and later on the farm had completely done away with the silks and satins, the embroidered weskits, and all the fripperies and fopperies of the gentleman of fashion beyond the Atlantic. The styles of the ladies came indubitably from Paris, but there is a sturdy American flavor about the clothes of our men. Whiskers may come and whiskers may go. Pants legs be loose and pants legs be tight. But that change of styles in a man's clothes is connected with courtship would be a hard point to disprove. He wants to look well for her—he wants to make an impression on her. It's as much in his blood as strutting before the hens is in the blood of a rooster.

Sports and Amusements

RUNNING AND WALKING MATCH, 1874

As far back as the fifties complaints began to be heard that the city dwellers were suffering from a lack of outdoor sports. The medical profession were the first to call attention to this flaw in our national development. Nor was the call unheeded. It met with a ready response from a people whose attitude toward physical exertion had been greatly influenced by the tradition of the frontier. Already restless under the restraints of city living, they showed an eagerness for sports which provided, if not active participation, at least an escape valve in the cheering from the grandstand.

For a decade, however, there was more talk than accomplishment, and it was not until the return of the soldiers after the Civil War that the great outdoors began to come into its own. Hardened by their strenuous campaigns, the returned soldiers craved exercise and the spirit of conquest.

Among the earliest sports to catch the public attention at this time were the running and walking matches. Considering themselves authorities on both these subjects, the soldiers not only indulged in the contests themselves, but followed the winners from one contest to another, supporting them, cheering them, and backing them with the bonus money that was burning a hole in their pockets. These foot contests had not yet become the semihumorous "bunion derbies" of later years but could stir up as much excitement as a present-day World Series.

Their avid interest in sports provided the urge for the startling development of baseball, football, and other competitive sports. They grew rapidly from the tiny realm of individual initiative into the big business they have become today, packing a million-dollar stadium or arena with cheering crowds at ringside prices as high as one hundred dollars a seat.

THE GAME OF CROQUET was a handy device for the ladies to get out into the open. "Of all of the epidemics that have swept our land," exclaimed one of the papers, "the swiftest and most infectious is croquet." Every lawn from the Atlantic to the Mississippi seemed to have been pressed into service. This was the first of the outdoor games that the men and women could enjoy together. Coming from England, the game soon reached a broader public—temporarily at least—than baseball. It was also a game which women could understand, a statement which can hardly be made about the great national pastime of today. For the ladies croquet furnished the first real breaking away from embroidery. As a form of exercise it was not, to be fair, much more vigorous than plying the needle and thread, but it did take the players out in the open air, and it permitted the ladies to show their gracefulness in holding and using the mallet. And while it may be ungentlemanly to speak of such a thing, it furnished a very charming excuse for the display of pretty ankles.

It was for that reason frowned upon by some of the purists in the pulpit, though the best people refused to listen and went merrily to Hell with a croquet mallet in hand, cheating a little perhaps, but having a very good time.

SKATING too had become quite a favorite sport among the ladies, in spite of the risk of a loss of dignity—and perhaps modesty. It gave them something to do outdoors when they could no longer play croquet. Skating was seized upon by the advocates of women's rights as a means of ushering in a day of greater independence, possibly because it is a sport which requires independence if the devotee is to remain upright; or perhaps it was because the sport furnished so excellent an argument for dress reform, and especially along the lines of a bloomer costume. But winter skating was not enough, and in the midst of the Civil War one James L. Plimpton introduced the roller skates. They were particularly welcome in the city where the youth was hampered by the absence of natural streams. The use of these tricky contrivances was at first confined to the upper classes, but like everything good they eventually reached the masses and in so large a way that no town was too small to have its rink.

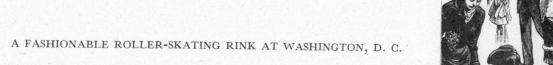

A FASHIONABLE ROLLER-SKATING RINK AT WASHINGTON, D. C.

BOWLING IN AMERICA goes back to the days of Rip Van Winkle and Sleepy Hollow. There was a green in downtown New York where the Dutchmen played the game while the city was still being called New Amsterdam. It was not exactly a ladylike game. Yet women tried their hand at it. Their participation in men's sports was really an important step toward freedom, both from the dictates of fashion and social etiquette.

The rise of women's colleges marked another distinct advance, for there the physical as well as the intellectual development was stressed. Girls were taught to love the outdoors. They were encouraged in boating and skating and tennis. They were furnished with bows and arrows and were taught archery, which, though a mild form of pastime, at least took them out in the open. For these recreations the hoop skirt, the crinoline, and the bustle were impossible. Garments and habits suited to the various sports necessarily followed, and in time the dress of women underwent a complete streamlining.

THE UNICYCLE, invented by an ingenious Yankee named Hemmings, was one of those devices designed to answer man's eternal quest for faster locomotion. This was in 1869, the same year in which the two-wheeled contraption called the bicycle was successfully produced in America. Within another decade the two-wheeled bicycle had gone up in the world with a big wheel in front and a little one in the rear. Stage acrobats took it up for entertainment purposes and, without realizing what they were about, contributed greatly to its popularity. It was indeed an acrobat named Hanlon who marketed the first successful bicycle in this country, and soon the roads and sidewalks of American cities were crawling with sports enthusiasts riding high.

PEDESTRIAN IN MAD DASH TO ESCAPE A BICYCLE ENTHUSIAST ON PENNSYLVANIA AVENUE IN WASHINGTON, D. C., 1884

So long as they ran on iron tires the bicycles were both noisy and uncomfortable. They were quite generally known as "boneshakers" until along in the eighties when they were equipped with rubber tires. Then their popularity advanced with great rapidity, especially after the dropped frame had put the cyclist back on the ground. Indeed, there were so many of them on the streets that in all the larger cities a force of "bicycle cops" had to be formed to keep the riders from exceeding the speed limits and becoming "scorchers." In the early part of the Gay Nineties the bicycle became the symbol of the new age of courtship, for, after all, a bit of diligent pedaling would carry a rider far from the Victorian parlor into the great outdoors.

THE SPEED LIMIT—A LAST WARNING

SPECTATOR SPORTS were something that came about slowly and naturally. In the beginning the games and contests were played for the amusement of the participants only. They were playing for the fun of it, for the exercise, or just for something to do. Idlers and passers-by stopped to watch them. In the cities with their vast populations there are always people who work at irregular times and who go out looking for a little amusement during their off hours. And always there are loafers standing around to see what they can see. The idle onlookers, appearing to be gentlemen of leisure, were called the "fancy," and it is to this designation that we are indebted for "fan" in current use. It was this large and easily entertained audience that was exploited so cleverly by Mr. Barnum with his freaks and curiosities and eventually with the "Greatest Show on Earth."

HIGH SOCIETY, keeping aloof from any sort of free entertainment such as occupied the loafers, provided exclusive entertainment for itself, at which for a long time the public was refused admittance—horse races, boat races, gymkhanas, and the like—until they discovered that the audience was really more important than the players and that to get the best players they must have the largest audiences.

JUDGMENT! JUDGMENT! HOW THE
UMPIRE MAY YET BE COMPELLED
TO DEFEND HIMSELF

Along with their guns and their knapsacks the
soldiers brought back from the Civil War a real love for
the game of baseball. The clubs in attendance at the
meetings of the American Association numbered nearly
a hundred in 1865 and double that number a year later.
"Since the war it has run like wildfire," one of the papers
declared editorially.

By 1872 baseball was hailed as the national game
of the country. And it was Mark Twain who explained
all this by declaring that it was "the very symbol, the
outward and visible expression of the drive and push
and rush and struggle of the raging, tearing, booming
nineteenth century."

But it was more than that. It was something that
any number could play, it was fun, and any old sandlot
would do for a diamond. Gradually the best players
found their way into the big leagues; and business,
noting the widespread interest, was not long in taking
over. The World Series games excite almost as much
interest as a presidential election—and sometimes more.

FOOTBALL MATCH BETWEEN YALE AND PRINCETON, 1879

As a spectator sport football probably stands at the top of the list. Of the persons who go to make up the gigantic crowds which jam to overflowing every stadium in the land, comparatively few ever play or ever have played the game. It is not like baseball in which every male with two arms—or even one—fancies himself as another Babe Ruth or Christie Mathewson. Not every man has the brawn required for football, or the weight or the speed or the determination, but if he has the price of admission he can become a first-class spectator.

The picture by A. B. Frost was drawn in 1879. Baseball was a rough, tough game then, and though it has adopted many changes in the rules, it is still a rough, tough game. Indorsed by Theodore Roosevelt as one of the exponents of his "strenuous life," it received his blessing at a time when it was being severely criticized as a menace to life and limb. Though formerly a kicking game resembling soccer, it was changed in the seventies to a form of Rugby and a disposition of forces and the use of strategem not unlike that employed in the roughest of all games—war.

THE BOOKMAKERS.

BACKING - THEIR FAVORITE

AFTER THE RACE — A WINNER

MESSENGER BOYS ARE ALLOWED 10 CENTS FOR BUYING AND 15 CENTS FOR CASHING TICKETS. KEEP FENCE

SCENES AT SHEEPSHEAD BAY RACING COURSE

Horse racing has well been named the Sport of Kings, for as a pastime it runs into big money. In pioneer days it was a sport in which anyone with a horse could participate. Entries at the old-time county fairs were almost entirely from the neighborhood. Entry fees were small, and since they were pooled to make up the stake, the winnings were more of an honor than a fortune. In time, however, fast horses began touring the fairs, working up larger stakes and cleaning out the yokels who had fast horses, or thought they had. Indeed, the incidence of the "dark horses" had a large part in bringing the sport into ill repute.

George Washington was not the only president who loved to see the horses run. Even the thrifty and academic John Quincy Adams used to slip off for an afternoon with the ponies.

Though horse racing was frowned upon and discouraged during the Civil War, it attained a new popularity immediately after the peace when taken up by the leaders of fashion in New York. Backed by wealthy sportsmen, the American Jockey Club purchased a beautiful site of some two hundred thirty acres in Westchester County which was named Jerome Park. Here a grandstand was erected to seat some eight thousand persons. The park was a success from the first, and it showed the way for the numerous other tracks which have sprung up all over the country.

COACHING never attained anything like national standing, yet it added a bit of color to life in the metropolitan area during the closing decades of the century and afforded the horse a chance to disport himself with a spectacle of the greatest magnificence before being completely eclipsed by the arrival of the automobile. For the masses the coaching parade was just another free show like the circus, the mummers, or a much abbreviated Mardi Gras. For society it was quite another matter, for not only did it give the socially secure a chance to flaunt their wealth and position, but it afforded to the parvenu an opportunity to show what he could do with his money and how well he could keep up with the parade.

DANCE-HALL BALLET GIRL

The sporting crowds were loyal supporters of the theater in all its branches. Indeed in boxing and wrestling it is often difficult to tell where the sporting event ends and the theatrical commences. As far back as 1876 there were sixteen theaters in New York. Taking them from south to north in the order of their location they were the Stadt, the Bowery, Niblo's, Theatre Comique, the Olympic, Lina Edwin's, the Globe, Wallack's, Union Square, the Academy of Music, the Fourteenth Street, Booth's, the Grand Opera House (at Eighth Avenue and Twenty-third Street), the Fifth Avenue, the St. James, and Woods'.

Aside from legitimate theaters there were night spots of every description on lower Broadway and the Bowery—establishments that catered to a rather mixed audience. The rise of the concert saloons in this neighborhood alarmed puritanical circles. But the illuminated transparencies and above all the pretty waitresses and show girls were a point of attraction for city people and out-of-towners alike. It was said that after the Civil War show business enjoyed a tremendous boom, with something like six hundred concert saloons in the Big City.

The interest taken by audiences in the performances was tremendous. People had their favorites for whom they stood up—and for whom they were sometimes knocked down. In 1849 a fight between the admirers of Macready and the Edwin Forrest enthusiasts grew to the proportions of a riot which had to be quelled by the militia.

We are told that the pay of the performers ranged from fifteen to fifty dollars a week, with some of the leading ladies and gentlemen receiving as much as one hundred or even two hundred dollars, while the ballet girls received only from eight to fifteen dollars a week, which may explain why they were so willing to meet people and accept invitations to go out to supper.

Up in the Galleries of the downtown theaters of old New York there was an air of informality, with the populace very much a part of the show. Their approval was vociferous and noisy, and their disapproval was something no actor cared to face. An uptown audience might leave the theater indignant and muttering, but downtown the enraged patrons would mob the place, throwing fruit and vegetables at the performers and tipping over and smashing the benches on which they were supposed to sit. Standing on the benches and spitting on the stage or into the boxes was a common occurrence, and even at Niblo's if a patron stood his top hat in the aisle during a performance it was almost certain to be used as a spittoon by other patrons attired with less formality. Indeed, any kind of marksmanship at a tall hat was at this time considered the height of humor. And patrons sitting in the orchestra pit of a theater were subjected to a steady rain of objects dropped from the gallery. These ranged from wadded up bits of paper and programs to bits of chewing gum and even quids of tobacco.

THE WESTERN DRAMA

Though the theatrical center of the nation was in New York, interest in the stage radiated over the entire country. Activity in recreating the semblance to life was almost as great as that in creating the real thing. As early as 1815 a touring company had traveled by wagon from Albany to the headwaters of the Allegheny River and downstream in small boats to the Ohio. It touched at Pittsburgh; Frankfort and Lexington, Kentucky; made a stopover at Cincinnati; and went on by boat as far as New Orleans. Later on, as the West developed, traveling troupes barnstormed through mud and rain from one mining camp to another, giving their performances in barns, saloons, bordellos, or any other place where a crowd could be gathered. Many of these performances were given without an admission fee, gratuities to the actors—and actresses—coming in the form of nuggets and pokes of gold dust thrown to the stage by drunken miners and others with an inebriated appreciation of art and pulchritude.

THE OPENING OF THE METROPOLITAN OPERA HOUSE in 1883 provided a fashionable hangout in which society could see and be seen, though not all the box holders had any great appreciation of music. Indeed the conversation in the boxes threatened to become a public scandal. Soundproof loges, constructed not unlike the showcases on Fifth Avenue, were suggested by *Puck* as a means of alleviating the annoyance of the music lover.

THE MINSTREL SHOW, now given over to the volunteer fire departments and other ama-
teurs, was once a very popular form of entertainment. Originating in America in the early part
of the nineteenth century it had its greatest vogue after the Civil War when the returning
soldiers began to carry the songs and drolleries of the colored people all over the country. For
many years these shows were given by white performers in blackface, all-man shows with an
all-man audience. Eventually, however, the colored folk took over their own show, producing
some of the finest comedians and endmen that minstrelsy was ever to know. In form the
Minstrel Show changed fundamentally during its declining years, when variety acts almost
entirely supplanted the singing.

THE DIME MUSEUMS existed only by preying upon the gullibility of their patrons, who were almost exclusively out-of-towners who had come to the Big City for amusement and lacked the means or taste for attending the theaters and other forms of entertainment of the better sort. While these small-time cheats did occasionally show a genuine bearded lady or a sword-swallower, most of their freaks were palpable frauds, and their places were hangouts for pickpockets, confidence men, and flimflammers of various sorts.

Mr. Barnum, after making a somewhat spectacular success with his museum of freaks and anomalies in New York, began enlarging his show by adding menageries as well as bands of itinerant acrobats. His exhibition, labeled as great moral entertainment, was described as an "Academy of Object Teaching." In the city his performances were given in the Hippodrome on Fourth Avenue above Twenty-seventh Street. The building, constructed in the form of a circus tent, was lighted by gas and heated by steam coils. And though his career in the amusement business had begun in 1835 it was not until 1871 that his "Greatest Show on Earth" was organized to tour the country on trains instead of by wagon. It was a colossal, a stupendous, a magnificent success.

P. T. BARNUM'S NEW AND GREATEST SHOW ON EARTH!

My great Traveling Centennial Academy of Object Teaching cost a million and a half of dollars, employs 1100 persons, 600 horses and ponies, and will be transported East to Maine and West to Missouri on 100 solid steel railroad cars. It by far surpasses all my former efforts; consists of sixty cages of rare wild animals and amphibia, including Barnum's $25,000 *Behemoth*, the only HIPPOPOTAMUS in America; vast Centennial Museum of living Mechanical Automata and other curiosities; a CENTENNIAL PORTRAIT GALLERY; BEST CIRCUS IN THE WORLD. A JUBILEE of Patriotic Song and Splendor; superb Historical Tableaux; National Anthems by several hundred trained voices, accompanied by music and roar of cannon; *the whole audience to rise and join in singing the national hymn,* "*America.*" I carry my own park of Cannon and a large Church Bell, fire a national salute of 13 guns each morning, accompanied by the public bells, and give the most extensive and gorgeous STREET PAGEANT ever witnessed, glittering with patriotic features, and attended by three bands of music. Each night a grand display of Patriotic Fireworks, showing WASHINGTON, American Flags, &c., in national colors of fine red, white, and blue, fine Balloons, &c. You will never see the like again. Admission to all, 50 cents. Children under nine, Half Price. P. T. BARNUM.

GILMORE'S PARADE

American musical taste of the seventies and eighties ran largely to the unusual, the sensational, and especially to the grandiose. The bigger the musical project the greater the appreciation and enthusiasm of the public. Recitals by a single artist were not well received even though the performer was at the top of his profession. It was suggested to the great Anton Rubenstein while touring in the South that he blacken his face to give him more the appearance of a minstrel. A noted Polish pianist was advertised to play four hundred notes in a single measure, and another was billed to play with his fists and elbows, and even with a walking stick.

The effort at this time was to produce the greatest rather than the best. A music festival to be successful must be gigantic, and an orchestra must be billed as the largest ever assembled. Even conservative Boston went overboard for bigness. At a peace festival shortly after the end of the Civil War a chorus of 1,000 voices was advertised as the main attraction, under the direction of Patrick S. Gilmore, an Irishman from Dublin. Apparently, however, the effort was not gigantic enough, and in 1872 a second peace festival was promulgated with a chorus of 20,000 and an orchestra of 2,000. Once more Gilmore was in charge, and in the Anvil Chorus he quite outdid himself with 100 Boston firemen pounding on real anvils to give the desired volume. He even resorted to the firing of artillery to increase the noise and thereby aroused the applause of some 40,000 persons who were brought to their feet with cheers.

ONE HUNDRED BOSTON FIREMEN PRACTICING FOR THE ANVIL CHORUS AT CHICKERING'S HALL

VIEWING "THE GREEK SLAVE," BY HIRAM POWERS

The Victorian cult of decency was, in the seventies and eighties, very much in the ascendency. Indeed, the period has been described as being "nasty nice." In the City of Brotherly Love the Academy had certain days for women only so that the fair sex might gaze upon plaster casts of the human body without being embarrassed by the presence of men who might be indelicate enough to notice what they were looking at. At the Art Museum in Boston a young lady who sold tickets was scolded by an outraged parson and told that she ought to be ashamed to be working in such a place. The Venus de Milo was almost the only undraped nude accepted in the American home without raised eyebrows from those who judged the beauty of statuary from the moral viewpoint.

WEEK ENDS AND VACATIONS were something very new even as late as the seventies. The working day in offices and manufacturing plants was ten hours long, and in the retail stores it was even longer, some of them advertising their eagerness to serve the public by remaining open until ten o'clock several nights a week. There were no merchants' associations at that time to agree upon an earlier closing hour, and there were as yet no well-organized workers' groups to take measures for obtaining shorter hours or better working conditions. Only the well-to-do were in a position to get away for a vacation, or even for a holiday. With the improvement of transportation, however, which made it possible to get to Coney Island and other resorts by horsecar and steamboat, the first faint glimmer of the week end appeared.

Some of the merchants began closing their stores Saturday evenings, and even Satuday afternoons, and in time the half-holiday became almost universal. With this tiny bit of leisure as a starter, excursions up the river and down the bay began to develop until the Saturday and Sunday crowds overwhelmed every craft that would float and every car that the transportation lines could muster. At this time there were no vacations with pay; there were, in fact no vacations. Those were to await a later and perhaps a better day.

ANNUAL EXCURSION OF THE EMPLOYEES OF FRANK LESLIE'S PUBLISHING HOUSE TO ORIENTAL GROVE.

THE STEAMBOAT LINES began to make their excursion trips up the Hudson as tempting as possible. They provided music and other means for fun and relaxation. They took their passengers not only for a ride but let them go ashore at attractive picnic grounds where they would wander amid the beauties of nature and picnic under the trees from the baskets all were permitted to carry. These excursions into the green became so popular that they were taken up by political clubs and district organizations as a means of getting better acquainted with the voters and holding them in line. The fate of many an aspirant for mayor and even for governor of the state has been settled at a clambake or a fishfry. Some of the most famous of these clambakes became annual affairs almost as important and far more corrupt than many of the conventions and caucuses, most of which were conducted and controlled from the well-known smoke-filled room not far away.

BEACHES ALONG THE ATLANTIC, both on the Jersey shore and the south shore of Long Island, became immensely popular and began an era of boom development. Summer hotels were going up all along the shore. Cottages were being built by the people of moderate means, or perhaps by construction companies for the purpose of summer rentals. The well-to-do desiring to avoid crowds bought large tracts of land on which they erected villas.

FASHION'S LATEST FOLLY

The vast popularity of the seashore was not long in bringing about a change of fashions in beach apparel. Previously the mere fact that men and women swam in the same ocean had put the legion of decency on their guard, and propriety had demanded in a loud voice that all swimmers, both male and female, should be completely dressed. The men had rebelled at the idea of wearing stockings but otherwise were completely clothed, enough to hamper them greatly in the matter of swimming. The pants of the men's bathing suits hung to their knees, and even further after they had become wet. Even the children were completely swathed in clothing.

SARATOGA TRUNK

Once America had learned to play it went into the matter with its usual exuberance for anything new. Never a land of moderation, it was soon overdoing the relaxation fully as much as it had previously underdone it. The shore was well enough for the hot months of summer, but

for spring and fall there had to be somewhere else to go, and the spas and watering places were discovered by the upper crust and were soon all the rage. Drinking the waters became as much a fad as swimming in them had been. And Saratoga, being the watering place nearest to New York and most easily accessible both by boat and by train, underwent a tremendous boom. Huge hotels sprang up along the main street of the little town, and smaller hotels and boarding houses were tucked into every available corner.

The gayest of toilettes were *de rigeur* in the palatial hotels. The style of never wearing the same gown twice regardless of the length of stay presented a real problem in the matter of baggage, which was finally solved by the invention of the so-called "Saratoga trunk."

THE LANCERS

GRAND UNION HOTEL, SARATOGA

Before the war the watering places had been highly respectable resorts, patronized for purposes of health only; but now they had suddenly become the playgrounds of wealth and society. War profiteers and ward heelers went swarming to Saratoga along with the grand dames of high society. Gamblers with their huge diamond shirt studs peopled the corridors and the verandas, exchanging hot tips on the latest railroad merger.

COMMODORE VANDERBILT IN SARATOGA

IN THE MOUNTAINS

The spas and mineral springs were not, however, for the people of modest means. They were geared for free spenders with fat purses. The patronage of vacationers with small means was not encouraged, and still having a holiday to spend, the white-collar workers and dwellers of the side streets in the city began to seek out country boarding houses and low-priced lodgings in the mountains. It was thus that the city dweller rediscovered the beauties of nature and the placid joys of the quiet countryside and were newly imbued with a love of the outdoors and the rural surroundings that had once characterized the American way of life.

ARRIVAL OF CITY BOARDERS AT A COUNTRY FARM HOUSE—A MUTUAL INSPECTION

People from the grass roots were not long in taking advantage of the new trend, and in the country districts within easy reach by rail of the large cities the crop of summer boarders brought more money to the rural population than any of the products growing on their broad acres. And many a farmer who had barely been able to eke a living from a hard-scrabble hillside came into a prosperous business of "taking in" summer boarders.

THE TRAVELING PHRENOLOGIST IN THE WHITE MOUNTAINS. "YES MISS, YOU HAVE A VERY REMARK-
ABLE HEAD—VERY."

FRESH MILK

With the coming of city boarders to the country the shoe was on the other foot. Usually it had been the country man who went to the city to be tricked and cheated at every turn. There were naturally some old scores to be paid off, but it was not long before the mutual distrust changed to friendship and furnished the city children especially with a new world and gave them a new idea of the importance of growing things. As they saw the earth turned and made ready for planting they greeted the green shoots coming out of the ground as something not wholly unexpected. They rejoiced in the harvest as something that mankind had actually helped to produce. Gradually they learned to value and love the simplicity of country ways, taking back to the city with them memories that were in many cases to cause profound changes in their way of living.

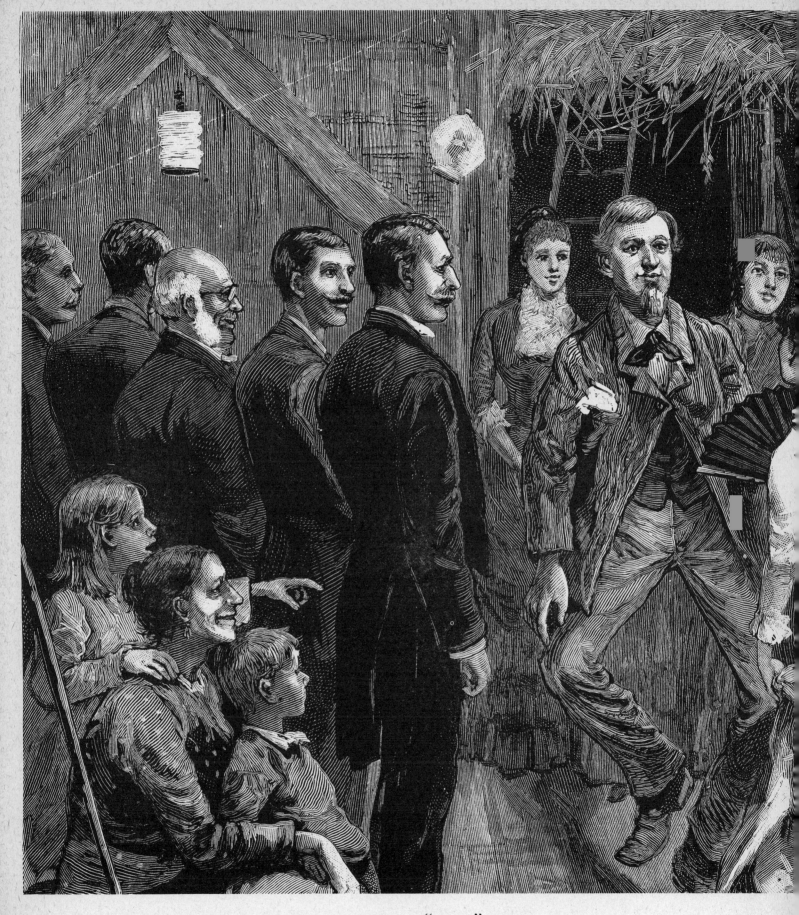

AN INCIDENT OF SUMMER BOARDING-HOUSE LIFE—A "SWELL" HOP IN A BARN

NO TIME FOR TOLL

History has a way of being a little ridiculous, especially at a hidden turn in the road where humanity cannot see far enough ahead to suspect that important developments are in the making. The first horseless carriage elicited howls and shouts of laughter from the sidewalks, as well as sarcasm and abuse from the farmer whose horse was scared into leaping fences and climbing trees. Only the crazy inventors who built the contraptions were smart enough to see that the story of highway transportation was about to enter into a phase where the horse would participate only as a unit of measurement.

But it is doubtful whether Duryea or Ford, or any of the early motor-car men realized that the puffing little "buggyaut" that was causing all the laughter was leading one of the greatest caravans of history, a vast migration which would carry people back from the city to the farm, thereby completing the cycle which had started from the farm to the city in the wake of the Civil War.

Nor would it have been imagined in the middle nineties that within a half-century both the farmer and the city dweller would be so completely mechanized and motorized that the buggy-wheel, the horse-collar, and the hitching-post would serve no useful purpose, save as collectors' items.

A BRIEF NOTE

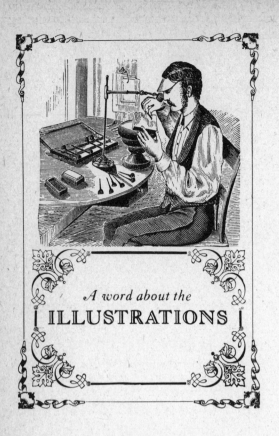

A word about the
ILLUSTRATIONS

The mid-nineteenth century was a period bristling with news of an ever-expanding nation. There was a keen sense of curiosity among the people; they longed for a mirror that would enable them to see themselves grow. The graphic arts answered this demand. They brought visual news to town and countryside. Woodcuts, lithographs, and photographs captured events, inventions, and personalities for the multitude to see.

In any survey of graphic reporting, Currier and Ives take first place. Their lithographs give us a glowing picture of the contemporary scene. They created untold delight as decorations in humble homes the country over. However, they were not really carriers of news for all. Manual methods were used exclusively in their manufacture; no means existed by which these pictures could be put on a mass-production basis.

The same is true of the new and startling art of photography which had its inception in the nineteenth century. Matthew Brady's pictures offer unmatched revelations of personalities and events. Yet, at the time of their appearance, these photographs defied reproduction in magazines. The age of the half-tone was still far away.

The American people as a whole witnessed their own history, saw their own opinions, peeves, and enthusiasms, reflected in the rough and ready delineations of the woodcut.

While some early photographs were transferred onto wood, most illustrations were based on pencil sketches by artists close to the pulse of the times and the people. Transposed to a woodblock, the line drawing could be made, without further ado, a part of the printed page. Words and pictures were printed on power-driven presses speedily and economically.

TRANSPOSED TO A WOODBLOCK,
THE LINE DRAWING COULD BE
MADE A PART OF THE PRINTED PAGE

It was in this field of pictorial journalism that the American genius revealed itself most tellingly during the second half of the nineteenth century. The host of popular magazines like *Harper's Weekly, Leslie's Illustrated Newspaper*, and many other pictorial publications—scientific, religious, and agricultural—gave the people of that time an impressive picture of their own world. These illustrations were far from arty. They were simple, truly democratic expressions of the spirit of the times. They showed Americans America as Americans fancied America to be.

Providing an insight into our own past, they are invaluable. The whole gamut of life— private and national—seems to radiate from these images. While their message has been supplemented by other types of illustrations, the authors of this volume have found it advisable, in the interest of a truly unified picture, to retell a part of the American story through the medium of contemporary woodcuts.

It is obvious that this panorama cannot be complete. No picture—not even a thousand pictures—can recreate a period. Pictures are merely peep-holes, offering a segment of reality. Yet these glimpses will, we hope, give the reader a feeling of the five fateful decades that will forever be a source of inspiration as we move toward an uncharted future.

A WARM RECEPTION AWAITED
THE ARRIVAL OF THE FAMILY
PAPER AT THOUSANDS OF FIRESIDES

INDEX